338
.109
71
Gia

‛01449

Giangrande, Carole, 1945–.
    Down to earth : the crisis in Canadian farming /
Carole Giangrande. –– Toronto : House of Anansi
Press, c1985.
    196 p. ; 22 cm.

Includes bibliographical references and index.
02767309   ISBN: 0887841473 (pbk.) :

1. Agriculture – Canada. 2. Agriculture – Economic
aspects – Canada. 3. Agriculture and state – Canada.
I. Title.

By the same author:

The Nuclear North: The People, the Regions and the Arms Race
(Anansi, 1983)

DOWN *to* EARTH
The Crisis In Canadian Farming

Carole Giangrande

ANANSI
Toronto   Buffalo   London   Sydney

Author photograph: W. Edward Hunt
Cover design: Laurel Angeloff
Front cover photo courtesy of the Agricultural Picture Service of the Central Office of Information, London.

Published with the assistance of the Canada Council and the Ontario Arts Council, and printed in Canada, by

House of Anansi Press Limited
35 Britain Street
Toronto, Ontario M5A 1R7

Canadian Cataloguing in Publication Data

Giangrande, Carole, 1945—
    Down to earth: the crisis in Canadian farming

Includes index.
ISBN 0-88784-147-3

1. Agriculture—Canada.   2. Agriculture—Economic aspects—Canada.   3. Agriculture and state—Canada.   I. Title.

S451.5.A1G73 1985   338.1'0971   C85-099319-9

For my parents.

Acknowledgements

My overview of farming in Canada could not have been undertaken without helpful contributions from many people and organisations. I would like to thank the Canada Council, the Ontario Arts Council and Therafields Foundation for their generous financial assistance which helped me complete this book. I would also like to acknowledge the years of assistance I received from my former colleagues at the CBC whose expertise in farming and farm broadcasting gave me a foundation from which to explore the vast enterprise of agriculture in this country.

Many farmers across the nation took time out from busy schedules to talk to me and to identify the most important problems and strengths of the farm community. I am very grateful for their observations, some of which helped me to point my inquiry in new and unexpected directions. In spite of their own troubles, these farmers showed me a hospitality and friendliness which added a warm personal dimension to my travels across the country. I would also like to thank James Polk, who helped me organise the diverse and often bewildering array of farm issues into a coherent whole. His encouragement and patience have been very much appreciated.

Finally, a word of thanks to my husband, Brian Gibson, whose friendship and interest in agriculture have added much to the enjoyment of writing this book.

Contents

Preface

For five years, I worked as an agriculture commentator for the CBC *Radio Noon* programme in Toronto. When I began that job, I was typical of most media people in my ignorance of agriculture. Fertilizer prices, grain exports, hog markets and the rising costs of feed all seemed to blur somewhere on the periphery of what I had liked to call "hard news." On the face of it, many of these concerns seemed relevant only to farmers, but as a public broadcaster, my job was to make agriculture stories as interesting to as many listeners as possible. Gradually, the mists cleared and what emerged were human faces, farmers whose job it was to feed us and who were among the most productive members of our society. Along with human faces came real sympathy. I saw the farmer's costs go up as he had to pay increasing amounts of money for fuel, machinery, and seed for spring planting. I was caught up in the interest-rate trauma of 1981, as the costs of borrowing money began driving farmers out of business. Newsworthy items were not hard to find: farmers told us that food prices at the supermarket were absurdly low, while market prices for cattle and hogs kept slipping. More and more farmers, caught between the high cost of borrowing and low prices received, were being wiped out.

In fact, in the 1980's, the farm economic crisis became severe enough to catch the attention of the "mainstream" media. In 1982, some desperate Ontario farmers banded together to resist foreclosures on their property, hoping to get the public attention they felt their plight deserved. The banks were apparently making big profits and driving farmers off their land. And where would all that foreclosed farmland end up? Would Canada, a prosperous, well-fed country, run out of land to feed itself? Gradually, media attention to the farmer waned as interest rates dropped and farm foreclosures stopped making headlines. Different farm stories now made news: drought, grasshoppers, crop-killing tornadoes and most tragically, famine in Africa. The headlines hinted at a world crisis, complex and difficult to resolve, and I began to feel that many of the statements made on the air by farm leaders were too pat. Money was touted as the answer to just about every farm problem. I realised that farming deserved the sort of reflection that goes beyond what a tightly-paced radio programme can offer: our daily package of assorted inter-views worked against a more comprehensive look.

The issues in the farm sector are broad and deep, eluding a media bias for dramatic events and "quick takes." What added to my unease was the sense that agriculture kept emerging on the air as a business and nothing more. How could we talk sensibly about the troubles of farming when we were examining only one small aspect of a vast human enterprise? I knew that Canadian farming was in a state of crisis; the facts about foreclosures, bankruptcies, soil erosion and low prices were repeated on the air day after day. But what I missed was the time to ask the more probing questions about the nature of this crisis. What exactly were its causes? Was it the fault of Canadian consumers who wanted the cheapest food available without being willing to face the consequences for the farmer? Or did the crisis point to the pressures of global markets, the influence of multinational corporations and the borrowing and lending policies of the banks? And what role did government play in the farmers' plight? Did the Canadian patchwork quilt of federal and provincial programmes help the farmer, or only support shoddy farm practices that needed to be scrutinized carefully? These, in turn, raised larger questions. Perhaps the doldrums of farming result from a dated style of agriculture which neither the farmer nor the environment can continue to afford. Should we continue to prop up high-tech agriculture with tax dollars, or should we start to insist that the farmer bite the bullet? Is it right to leave farming to the farmers? As a consumer—and gardener—I wanted to find out how urban people fit into the picture. Did *we* have a role to play in agricultural reform? Farmers had often told me what was wrong; now I felt that it was time to look at the farm crisis and see for myself.

Any farmer in Canada will tell you that his biggest problems are high interest rates, low commodity prices, the shrinking value of his enterprise—or a combination of the three. Agriculture has become a precarious business undertaking, even though it produces goods upon which all our lives depend. Modern agriculture is a business, but it is also a way of life and building-block of rural communities and values. As the farm economy is damaged, all of these social elements are also disrupted. It is because farming is such a complex activity that its problems are often so difficult to isolate and solve. In North America, for example, the idea of family farming is one which is rich in myth and tradition, a fact which often leaves today's high-tech, "businesslike" farmer somewhat uncomfortable about his image.

Over eighty percent of Canada's farms are owned, managed and operated by members of the same family[1] who are also the investors in their own business. Family farms come in all sizes, from the tiny forty-acre orchards in British Columbia's Okanagan Valley to the two-thousand acre prairie farms needed to grow grain and raise cattle. Size or lifestyle do not define a family farm. As an enterprise, they are at odds with corporate farming, which has gained a solid foothold in the United States, compared to a slim .4 percent of farms in Canada.[2] These so-called "factory farms" are owned and heavily capitalised by large corporations which count food as only one of their investments. A corporation appoints its own farm managers, but those who are employed in farming activities are, in fact, rural assembly-line workers who have no stake in the farm enterprise.

Nonetheless, the Canadian farm crisis involves, in part, a threat to the family farm as a unique rural institution, whose owners worked and managed their own business. In areas such as Ontario, farmers have spent the past ten years watching some of Canada's best farmland disappear in a wave of foreign investment and urban development. And while our farmers continue to produce huge amounts of food, they do so on a land base that is rapidly shrinking, either through intensive farming techniques that damage the soil, or through urban sprawl.

If you travel across Canada, you may find this hard to believe; we are a country known for under-population and for vast, empty spaces. But only eleven percent of our land is of any use for agriculture; out of that amount, only one-half of one percent qualifies as prime (Class 1) farmland.[3] Five percent of the total acreage is good for raising crops; the rest is useful only for pasture land. And our very best farmland sits under and around our large cities—including Toronto, Winnipeg, Edmonton, London and Montreal. More top-class land makes up the "urban fringes" in the lower Fraser and Okanagan fruitlands of British Columbia, Essex and Kent Counties in southwest Ontario's cash-crop belt, the Niagara fruitlands, the farmlands south of Montreal and in Nova Scotia's Annapolis Valley.

A recent Senate study points out that from one-third to one-half of Canada's Class 1 farmland is within a two-hour drive of Toronto.[4] If you want a graphic view of how serious this problem is, go to the top of Toronto's CN Tower. From there, you can see 37 percent of Canada's Class 1 farmland and over 25 percent of our Class 2 land—all of it within a short drive of the city of Toronto.[5] While our best farmland has declined sharply over the past twenty years, agriculture has expanded into the more fragile and less productive soils of the northern Prairies, where the weather can swing between extreme cold and drought. As the second-largest country in the world, we have croplands only as large as Sweden; all of our Class 1 farmland would fit comfortably into the province of New Brunswick.[6]

The remaining farmland is relatively costly, a major obstacle for the young farmer who must borrow heavily to go into business. And to pay for that land, he or she often ends up working it as intensively as possible, mono-cropping year after year in the hope of earning enough money to pay off a hefty debt. In looking at this pattern, I began to see another facet of the farm crisis. Today's large-scale agriculture begins with big capital expenses and costly inputs—farm machinery, chemical fertilizers and pesticides. In turn, these products rely directly or indirectly on expensive, petroleum-based fuels or chemicals. Farmers say they cannot operate their businesses without these inputs, and must borrow hundreds of thousands of dollars each year to keep producing. Before the energy crisis of the early Seventies, borrowing and interest rates were not major problems for them. Farmers were encouraged by provincial agriculture ministries and banks to expand their operations in order to make them more profitable and competitive.

By the late Seventies, farmers were hit by spiraling fuel and chemical costs and rising interest rates on both their mortgages and on the money they borrow yearly to finance their farm operations. Once the stereotype of the rugged individual, today's farmer is now completely dependent on the rising costs of energy, erratic interest rates and fluctuating prices for his crops and livestock. In short, he can no longer function as a farmer without the aid of banks and large corporations. As I thought about this, I was slowly beginning to see that something fundamental to our *idea* of the farmer has changed dramatically. And I sensed that there was much more to this farm crisis than many farmers or politicians were willing to admit.

As a broadcaster, I had interviewed many people who told me that the crisis on the family farm was the worst since the Depression of the 1930's. No one suggested to me that the seeds of this crisis may have been planted inadvertently, with the wholesale acceptance of large-scale industrial farming. But the economic problems involved in this style of farming have been driven to the surface largely because of the harsh economic climate of the past few years. In fact, the

figures are grim.   In 1983, when 488 farmers went bankrupt
across Canada, the Canadian Bankers' Association pointed
out that this was only a small fraction of Canada's three
hundred thousand farmers. The CBA added that other
bankrupt small businesses far outnumbered the farms that
failed in 1983.[7] But a year later, a survey conducted by
the federal Ministry of Consumer and Corporate Affairs
showed that 551 farms had gone bankrupt in 1984.[8] The
number of farm bankruptcies was clearly on the rise, with
no end in sight.

Ironically, the largest number of bankruptcies in 1984
happened in the two provinces where governments have
invested huge sums of money to help the farmer. In the first
three quarters of 1984, bankruptcies in Quebec jumped 78
percent; 127 farmers went out of business, compared to 74 in
the same period the previous year. The head of Quebec's
major farm organisation, Union des Producteurs Agricoles
(UPA) acknowledged that farm bankruptcies in his province
are well below those of other small businesses.[9] However,
Quebec farmers have been among the most heavily subsidised
in the country, because in the late 1970's, provincial agriculture minister Jean Garon set up a series of generous
farm assistance programmes aimed at establishing food self-
sufficiency in an independent Quebec. The politics have
now faded, and while the subsidies remain, they have, in
some cases, encouraged farmers to expand, only to get
thumped later with rising interest rates. Quebec's livestock
farmers were the hardest hit in 1984, with at least 70 farm
failures. Many of them were already hurt by poor red meat
prices, and the final blow was the high cost of feed after the
prairie drought.[10] Farmers in Alberta are also heavily subsidised by their provincial government, and yet bankruptcies in that province rose sharply in 1984. Their problem
dates back to the 1970's, when many young Alberta farmers
received low interest rates on government loans to help
them start in the business. Elmer Allan, the head of Unifarm,
Alberta's farm organisation, says many farmers paid too
much for land, expecting a rise in land values which never
came. Hard economic times, with some poor business management decisions, spelled the end.[11]

Many farm organisations believe that these bankruptcies don't account for the number of farm foreclosures pushed by the banks on operations that no longer appear profitable. Since the Bankruptcy Act only allows forced farm bankruptcies when the farm is incorporated, banks often use foreclosure to claim the funds they are owed by family farmers. The Ontario Federation of Agriculture estimates that for every voluntary bankruptcy, there are ten farmers squeezed out by foreclosure, not including farmers who quit the business before they lose all their equity.[12] If that arithmetic is correct, we are losing up to five thousand farmers a year during hard times. Are we threatened with a loss of food because of farm failures? Or are we just losing business people who were inefficient farm managers?

The banks insist that the vast majority of farmers continue to do relatively well; the Royal Bank of Canada's Agricultural Vice-President says that 95 percent of their farm borrowers pay their bills on time.[13] Crops and livestock are abundant in this country and no one born here has ever had to deal with empty shelves at the local supermarket. Not only is our food plentiful, but it is also relatively cheap. In Canada, we spend about 12 percent of our annual income on food[14] — the lowest percentage in the world, with the exception of the United States. (This discourages many farmers, who feel that their productivity has only helped to push down the price of food.) Despite our bounty, imports are on the rise; between 1961 and 1976, our food imports jumped in value almost seventy percent — from $854 million to $2,872 million.[15]

Cheap food means that Canadian farmers often earn less than their costs. The exceptions are farmers who work in the four areas regulated by national marketing boards — milk, eggs, chicken and turkey production. Thus farmers are leaving the business, and the farms remaining have grown in size. In 1951, Canada had 600,000 farms. Today, there are half that number. Since the 1950's, the amount of land used for farming has been steadily declining; between 1961 and 1976 (the period in which the most dramatic changes occurred), over three and a half million acres of land were lost to farming — an area about the size of Prince Edward Island.[16]

Former agriculture minister Eugene Whalen often used to say that "our farmers are the most efficient and productive in the world." "Efficiency" and "productivity" describe the values of today's farmer. They also happen to be the values of large-scale industry. Is that really what we are striving for in Canadian agriculture? Is that enough to keep the farmer going? The more I tried to find out about the farmers' malaise, the more I began to realise that the real crisis involved a broad area of social change which I could only glimpse as a farm broadcaster. If agriculture is, in fact, a building-block of society, then it has to involve the rest of us as well; the farmer's dilemma is, in some way, also ours. Farmers often say that our concern for them ought to be based on the fact that we all eat. True enough. But how should our concern be expressed? What do the farmers want?

There is still widespread media apathy about farming. Only farm disaster stories make headlines. I meet many otherwise well-informed urban people whose eyes glaze over when I talk about agriculture. Is this blasé attitude also a part of the crisis? Are we really dealing with complacent people who don't appreciate what it takes to keep a country well-fed? The farmer often thinks so, and with some justification. The consumer, the producer, the politician, the media— all seem to contribute to the crisis in agriculture, whatever the components of that crisis may be, if indeed there *is* a "crisis" in any urgent, specific sense. The more I thought about my media job and the signs of a larger disturbance in the agricultural world, the more I wanted to know. I decided to start with the basics and speak to the farmers in their own homes, away from the pressures of deadlines and radio "clips," to find out what they thought the troubles were. So, in the summer and fall of 1984, I left home for a series of trips through the back roads of rural Canada, where I had my chance to hear the farmer's own story.

Part I: The Farmers' Story

1
Ontario's Farm Crisis

Highway 427 at the west end of Toronto takes you north of
Highway 7, an east-west artery that marks the boundary
between northern Toronto and its rural fringe. Driving a
mile or so north of 7, you suddenly find yourself in the
country, and a few turns take you down the sideroads of the
area known as Caledon East, a small community which has
become home for many hobby farmers and former Toronto
residents. It was midsummer when I drove out there, and
everywhere I looked, the fields were full of corn and golden
barley, ready for harvest. I drove down a dirt road and
turned my car into a long, handsomely-treed laneway. As I
came closer to the farm, I could see the fields were full of
oats and barley; they were, without a doubt, the most attractive part of this particular operation. The farmhouse itself
looked a bit rundown and the barn in back appeared to be in
pretty bad shape from the road. John and Wanda King's
home is typical of rural Ontario, with its narrow, red brick
shape, and gingerbread gables and green wooden shutters.
The Kings are hospitable people who invited me to join

them in their living room for a cup of coffee. John is a big man with a beard; he was wearing his work clothes because he planned to cut hay after we finished talking. Wanda is plump, pink-faced and cheerful. Her husband had been farming for twenty-five years; she came to the farm and married him three years ago. They have two children. Their hectic lives are reflected in the state of their small living-room, crammed with various objects. A playpen with baby clothes and toys, couches, chairs, a woodstove and in the middle of the room, a big table with a lace tablecloth where we sat and talked. The walls were decorated with flowered paper and dark paneled wood, which added to the close feeling of the room. But for these people, their real world is outside in the fields.

John is a graduate of the Ontario Agricultural College at the University of Guelph, one of Canada's best-known agricultural schools. He now raises grain and beef, and because of this, he's had to face the same low prices for red meat and the same high interest rates that have put other farmers out of business. But John has one advantage that many others lack. His farm sits on one hundred acres of farmland which has inflated in value because it is located right on Toronto's urban fringe. This has boosted the equity of John's farm, and as a result, the bank doesn't worry when his cash flow dwindles; they are not concerned that their investment will erode in value. John is not at all sentimental about his attachment to the land. He has already severed off one lot and sold it to help finance the operation. I asked him if he would sell the rest if the price were right. "Yes, I would," he said emphatically. "There's more to farming than just a way of life," he added. "It's a business."

The Kings own one hundred valuable acres and they rent a few hundred more. This kind of arrangement is now common in Ontario. Farm sizes average 200 acres in this province, but most farmers rent additional land because they cannot afford to buy it. The reason for this goes back to the 1970's, when many urban speculators and foreign investors started buying good farmland in the northwest edge of Toronto, along the Niagara Peninsula and in the rich croplands of southwest Ontario. Land prices started going up as speculators gambled on the rezoning of these areas to industrial land. Several local citizens' groups have sprung up to fight these moves. But still, the local farmers who rent this land usually can't be sure if their annual leases will be renewed. And with the belief that the land will soon be paved over, it is easy to understand why farmers don't want to invest much money in soil conservation. In their own words, they don't farm the soil—they mine it. Corn dominates these rented fields and it is produced continuously year after year. Corn is one of the hardest crops on the soil; it drains it of nutrients and it needs large quantities of chemicals to keep it growing continuously. No crop rotations are used with corn to give the soil a break; a pasture crop would help the fields, but it would hurt farmers' incomes for the year in which it is grown.

John King has had financial difficulties, but both good equity and some skillful decision-making has helped keep him in business. In the winter when he isn't as busy, he spends more time calculating when he ought to buy and sell his cattle. Red meat producers can't guarantee what price they will get when the cattle are ready to go to market, so John does a little hedging on the futures market. This involves selling a contract to deliver his cattle at a future date, a move which allows him to "lock in" a guaranteed good price, protecting him if the price collapses by the time his cattle are ready to sell. However, John adds, "I've never had a year when I could say, 'I made money on beef and grain.'" He pointed out that the grain market in North America has been volatile for years. And weather also affects the price he gets for grain; 1983's hot, dry weather was bad for his crop, while in 1984, he had a record yield. But when everybody does well with good weather, there is the chance that large quantities of grain will push the price down for everyone.

With all these frustrations, it may be hard to believe that John and Wanda still want to farm. In any other business, consistently low prices and high costs would, at best, not be tolerated; at worst, they would force an owner out of business. But even for someone as practical as John King, farming means more than the cash return. When I asked him why he stayed in farming, he laughed out loud. "Insanity—stupidity!" he chuckled. Then he added, "Maybe because it's challenging and frustrating—and besides, I wouldn't like working for someone else." He enjoys what he feels is the independence of farm life; even with the economic strain, he is not too happy about plans for government stabilisation programmes to help out the beef industry. He echoes the attitude of many farmers in the red meat business when he says "Whenever you take something from government, you become more dependent." And he doesn't like proposals to regulate the industry so that the price and the supply of beef will be more stable. As a man in business for himself, he values his right to make his own buying and selling decisions and to take the risks that go along with them.

John and Wanda's comments about farm life reflect their concern with the farm economy. But like many farmers, they also wonder how they can tell the urban consumer about the problems they face. For Wanda, this issue strikes home; before she came to the farm, she lived in Toronto. Because of this, she knows what it is like to be ignorant of country life and she looks at it with a wry sense of humour. "To be honest," she said, "when John told me he was a farmer, I thought he just put the seeds in the ground and sat on the front porch and watched them grow!" Nevertheless, she is amazed at the misconceptions many of her friends have about farmers. "Many people think farmers get a free ride from the government," she said, "but then many people get these negative attitudes because they grew up on farms themselves." Because Wanda has been an urban consumer, she is in a good position to see both sides of the problem—and she is frank about it. "The fact is that if something from Mexico is cheaper, people will buy it. That means fruit and vegetables. Cheaper imports usually come in during our season (from the US and Mexico)." And while she understands that most people are more interested in the cost of a product than in where it comes from, she still feels annoyed. "You know, agriculture is so basic," she said. "There can't be anything more basic. Politicians can talk all they want, but if they don't have any food, they'll drop dead at the end of the day!"

Even though he knows he won't be farming in the Caledon area much longer, John still takes pride in what he can do while he is still here. "When I come home and I can say 'my grain was graded Number One at the elevator with no dockage'—that's exciting," he said, smiling. What discouragement the Kings may feel shows in their surroundings; they see no need to invest money fixing up the place when they don't even know how much longer they will be there. "But he'd be no fun to live with if he left farming," Wanda said, laughing. And for all the swings of the grain and cattle markets, those are the areas of farming that John likes best. "You stick with what you know,"he said matter-of-factly.

But while they think about the business, these two practical people talk about their work in ways that have little to do with dollars and cents. The Kings speak freely of their belief that some people have to be willing to stick to farming, whatever the hardships, because farmers help people get fed. This quiet moral attitude is one which many farmers share when they think about the value of their work. But it also makes their love of farming easy to exploit—in some cases, until they can't farm anymore. Ontario's Waterloo County is best known as the home of the Mennonites, a religious body whose farm members practice an older form of agriculture which stresses simple tools and small-scale technology. But the county also contains Guelph and Kitchener, two medium-sized neighbouring cities with many up-to-date resources for the commercial farmer—from the University of Guelph to the sprawling Kitchener-Waterloo Stockyards. The two cities are situated roughly eighty kilometres southwest of Toronto. And like Toronto, they have been gradually expanding into the surrounding countryside. I drove down 33 Sideroad to an attractive old farm at the end of a long laneway bordered by big shade trees. The farmhouse was built of stone and bordered by beds of bright red and pink impatiens flowers. In the back, there was a barn and a granary which also looked well cared-for.

John Brubacher came out of the house to meet me. He is a round-faced, well-tanned man, smiling and friendly. We sat down to talk under the big trees at the side of the house, facing the shed. It was a very hot day and this green and quiet spot felt almost idyllic. But it no longer belongs to John Brubacher. He and his family were among the many casualities in the red meat business. Two and a half years ago, the family corporation—made up of Brubacher, his brother and his brother-in-law—sold all of its assets. They once had twenty-eight hundred head of cattle on feed, plus fifteen hundred acres of feed grain—a fairly large spread for Ontario. On the original family farm in nearby Elmira, they raised twenty-eight thousand laying hens along with their own pullets (the chicks that grow up to be egg layers). The farm I was visiting was bought in 1975. The total value of their operation and their farm sales once ran in the multi-millions. But according to Brubacher, the jump in interest rates over an eighteen-month period hit them hard. Their losses were, in his words, "phenomenal." As he put it, "the cattle business was no good; that was a simple fact."

The corporation sold its assets to foreign investors from Germany; he has leased his farm back from them and he, in turn, sublets parts of it. While he doesn't actively farm himself, he has a thousand pigs on feed at another farm. He now holds a job at a feed mill; it is the first job he has ever held off the farm. Selling his assets to foreign investors didn't bother him. "They were a buyer," he said offhandedly; he believes that foreign investors help stabilise land prices while making the land more valuable. These buyers rent out the fields—and Brubacher adds that the investors who took over his place are "co-operative people" who are willing to let him have longer-term leases of up to five years.

In cases like this, it is hard to judge exactly what it was that pushed such a big farm over the edge. Perhaps they expanded too quickly, making poor buying and selling decisions at the wrong time. Sometimes the bank simply decides to call farm loans, ordering farmers to sell their assets because the equity of the business is eroding under the burden of debt. Many of these farmers feel that high interest rates are just not fair. Whatever the truth of the matter, Brubacher represents a type of young farmer who has had some long thoughts about the nature of his business. He served for two years on the executive of the Ontario Cattlemen's Association, the group that speaks for most cattle producers in the province. And in taking on this job, he became involved in the heart of a controversy that has polarised red meat producers across Canada: the dispute over supply-management in the red meat industry.

Simply put, supply-management is a system under which the amount of a product a farmer may produce is regulated to meet consumer demand. Farmers in Canada who produce milk, eggs, chicken and turkey all operate under this system. With supply-management, the farmer gets a quota—which is, in effect, a license to raise and sell a specific amount of food or livestock. The size of the quota is based on a farmer's production in the year before the system comes into effect. People who support supply-management say it guarantees the farmer a decent income, while the consumer gets a steady supply of goods all year round. Farmers who work under the system like the fact that supply-managed marketing boards have legal powers to set the price the farmer gets according to what it costs to produce the product. And because farmers break even under this system, we seldom hear about bankruptcies in the milk, egg or poultry business.

Getting a quota isn't always easy; over the years, it has acquired dollar value because of limited supply. But the system of supply-management ought to work well in a country such as ours where the small population can't consume the large supply of certain farm goods which sometimes flood the market and push the price down. And countries such as Canada which have signed the General Agreements on Tariffs and Trade (GATT) are allowed to ban imports that would compete with supply-managed products. With guaranteed prices and an orderly marketing system, we might expect that red meat producers would applaud the idea. But that has not been the case. Former agriculture minister Eugene Whalen pushed hard for supply-management in cattle and hogs; he even held a national referendum on the issue for beef producers, but his side narrowly lost. The Ontario Cattlemen's Association has voted on supply-management, but resolutions asking the OCA to study the system have failed to pass by narrow margins. For cattle producers who oppose supply-management, anathema would be a mild term to describe how they feel about it. "Socialism," "Marxism" and "government interference" are some of the printable terms that are frequently used to describe the system. At first glance, it is hard to understand the intensity of this feeling, since red meat producers have been so badly hurt by low market prices and fluctuating feed grain costs. But many farmers—including John Brubacher—now believe that opposition to supply-management comes from the type of person who likes to do business in a setting that can only be described as a free-for-all. The cattle trade may, in fact, be the most unregulated business in Canada, if not in North America.

It's hard for a farmer to determine what price he will get for his livestock when it finally goes to market, either as a young calf or as a thousand-pound fattened (or "finished") steer. Many uncontrolled variables help set that price—the cost of feed grain, the number of cattle on the market, consumer demand and transport costs.

The cattle business starts with the "cow-calf" operators on the big range lands of western Canada and the US. As their name suggests, these farmers produce only the calves, which are then shipped eastward to the feedlot operators who fatten them up for market. But there are more than calves and fat cattle on that market; steers can be bought and sold at any stage of the finishing process as "replacement" cattle when a producer needs more animals to augment a herd after some steers have gone to slaughter. Or heavy steers can be bought and sold on the "short-keep" market, where a cattle farmer can take a chance and buy an animal that is very nearly fattened up, knowing that if he sells it at the right time he can make good money, with very little investment in the feed and upkeep of the steer.

However confusing this market may appear to the rest of us, many cattle producers have, until recently, survived and made money under this system. At one time, an astute farmer could earn a reasonable living marketing his beef if he paid close attention to both the quantity of beef he produced and to the relatively stable "beef cycle"—the recurring pattern of high and low cattle prices. In a typical phase of this beef cycle, cow-calf farmers would earn more money at times when they produced just enough beef to meet the demand. As profits went up, both cow-calf and feedlot operators could increase their herds and this would force the price of cattle down again as the volume of meat on the market went up. Farmers would then cut back their herds and prices would remain low until the backlog of red meat was cleared off the market. Once again, farm-gate prices would rise as the farmer cut back the number of cattle to be sent for slaughter.

For a long time, this common-sense, supply-and-demand model worked reasonably well. It was helped along by the fact that, since the Second World War, North Americans have been big consumers of red meat. This allowed the demand for steaks and roasts to boost the price at the points in the cycle when the supply was cut back. The turning point came in the Seventies, as farmers began to cut back their herds, pushing up the price of beef. It happened at just the wrong time. The energy crisis was pushing up the price of fuel, which had a major effect on inflation and on the cost of all consumer goods, including food. High meat prices were an easy target for consumers who had to cut back somewhere as the economic squeeze started to hurt. The Sunday roast began to disappear from the Canadian dinner table, along with the demand for better quality cuts of red meat. Producers then wanted to expand their herds to help push the price down. But the high interest rates and the heavy operating costs of the late Seventies and early Eighties made the cattle build-up hard for many farmers to sustain. Instead, farmers started to cut back their herds once again to save money; this backfired as more beef ended up on the market and prices tumbled. The low prices pushed many farmers into bankruptcy, while others faced foreclosure when they couldn't meet the payments on their loans. The beef cycle was also disrupted by the fluctuation of grain prices. Normally when feed grain prices drop, farmers buy the cheaper grain and feed it to larger herds of cattle, but when grain prices rise, it becomes more costly to feed those cattle on hand. Even during periods when the beef cycle operated smoothly, the cattle producer had many factors to consider when deciding whether to buy or sell. But many cattle farmers now say that world conditions, including the effects of major grain sales and grain boycotts, have disrupted the beef cycle for good. Without a stable beef cycle, many other factors go into setting the market price for beef. Cattle can be marketed in any number of ways—through the public stockyards, through packers who buy finished cattle direct from the farmer or through video and electronic auction sales. All the different marketing systems and the number of cattle sold through them can effect the market price for cattle over a period of days or weeks. Feed grain costs, naturally, can be bounced around by the weather, federal policy on big grain exports, exchange rates on the dollar and the often-murky international politics of the grain trade and the futures market.

It may not be surprising, then, when producers such as John Brubacher find themselves suddenly squeezed out of the business. And yet, one of the things that attracts people to the cattle market is the ability to choose this high element of risk. Many cattle producers see the trade as the last bastion of old-fashioned free enterprise, where the entrepreneur alone buys and sells when and how he pleases. For some, the big gamble has paid off. For many others, it has meant bankruptcy, foreclosure and the rueful comment you often hear from farmers that "free enterprise means you're free to go broke." It is hard to know if a payoff in the cattle market involves skill or luck when farmers have relatively little control over the economic environment in which they have to conduct their business—including energy costs, inflation and high interest rates.

John Brubacher talks about all this with a sense of irony, as he remembers how he tried to bring home the plight of many beef producers to the executive of the Cattlemen's Association. Like many other farmers, he believes that in Ontario, it is almost impossible to get beef producers to work together or to organise themselves politically. "There is a different type of individual in beef," he said thoughtfully. "It attracts people who are competitors, gamblers—real cowboys." According to him, they don't realise the advantages of setting up a quota system together; co-operation is apparently not their style. But he thinks that in another generation of cattle farmers, these attitudes may change, "Kids don't see as many cowboy movies on TV as we did," he says, "But the competitive scenario still holds today."

Although he doesn't expect supply-management for some time, Brubacher thinks that the red meat industry will gradually become more regulated. He points to the negotiations that have taken place over the last few years between the federal government and the provinces of Ontario, Manitoba, Saskatchewan and Alberta; they plan to set up a red meat stabilisation programme to help farmers who get low cattle prices in a poor year. Trying to impose some order on the cattle market has become almost an occupational hazard for anyone who makes a move. In early 1984, Ontario's former agriculture minister, Dennis Timbrell proposed a "single selling desk" system for cattle. While not a supply-managed marketing board, this would have helped stabilise prices by offering all producers equal access to the same markets at the same time.[1] But had the province succeeded in setting up such a central desk, it would have undercut the power of the staunchly free-enterprise Ontario Cattlemen's Association as the voice of the province's beef producers. The response of the OCA to the proposed regulation was so hostile that Mr. Timbrell gradually backed away from his plan. And while he had commissioned a six-month study on marketing alternatives, Mr. Timbrell finally dropped his plan altogether. In fact, the OCA had been so incensed by the attempt to regulate the cattle market that they successfully lobbied for his defeat in his close bid for Ontario's premiership in early 1985.[2] While about half the members of the OCA were angered by the provincial plan to stabilise beef prices, they are not at all opposed to the idea of receiving cash payments from Ottawa or the provinces as subsidies when beef prices drop too low.

For farmers like Brubacher, the marketing debate has been a good opportunity to reflect on where the red meat business is going. Without commenting directly on what had happened to him, he spoke slowly and thoughtfully about the relationship farmers have with the banks. His careful tone implied that he was speaking cautiously and in fact held strong views about the issue. "Ninety-five percent of farmers don't realise the power of the banks," he said quietly. "Forms can get passed over to you and when you are friendly with the banker, you may tend to trust him and just sign." I have heard farmers make this comment over and over again. No one likes to talk about their setbacks, and most farmers are too proud to go into all the painful details.

Selling the farm has led John Brubacher to a very different kind of life. For the first time, he has a regular job off the farm and a mere five-day work-week. His responsibilities stop when he comes home from work and, for now, he likes it that way. He has thought that at some future date he might put money into farming once again by investing with a group of farmers who would hire a manager to run the operation. But for now, he'd rather stay out of farming. On the day I visited he was at home alone. His wife and kids were away on an outing. As I left, I had the sense that he was somewhat lost without the farm business which had pre-occupied him for so long. I couldn't help feeling that this well-tended, restful farm seemed rather deserted and empty— except for the farmer who sat alone in the middle of all that land that was no longer his.

For many farmers, the business comes first, and when it goes, the farmer's life and the lives of his family unravel along with it. But it doesn't always turn out that way, as I found out when I spoke to John Langlois, a hog farmer in Ontario's Oxford County. I drove one afternoon along Highway 59, a north-south road running through the corn and tobacco country of southwestern Ontario. North of the town of Woodstock, County Road 97 takes you west to what looks like a well-kept rural home, the kind you see on the cover of farm magazines. A pair or twin silos and a red barn were visible from the laneway, and a horse was grazing in the pasture in front of the silos. Out in back, the fields were all full of grain. As I turned right into the laneway, I came to a large brick home with very tall front doors—a new building, not at all like the typical Ontario farmhouse. It's the home that John and Sue Langlois had built for themselves and their eight children. The attractive, split-level house has cream-coloured walls and comfortable, upholstered chairs in the living room. It feels prosperous and friendly. While we talked, Sue nursed her six-week old baby and some of the other kids wandered in and out of the room. The Langlois family raises hogs and beef cattle. They send five thousand hogs a year to market and they have a cattle feedlot with close to one hundred head of cattle. They used to raise more than that, but like many other farmers, they've been hit by poor red meat prices. They rent 600 of their 800 acres of land to raise cash crops—corn, soybeans, wheat and vegetables.

John is a dark-haired man with strong features and a steady gaze. He and his wife have been farming for twenty years. But the story he tells is an unusual one. He had grown up on a mixed family farm in the Windsor area and he left it for a university education and an academic career. "I had a couple of degrees hanging on the wall," he said. "Sociology, economics, and I had started my PhD. But I felt that all I would end up doing would be to perpetuate myself by teaching sociology to someone else, and so on. I had always loved farming. I couldn't deny it; above all, I wanted to farm. I really didn't want to do anything else." His education didn't stop him from getting caught in the economic squeeze. When I asked him how his farm was doing, he paused for a moment before he spoke. "Well, the last five years has hit us hard,"he said slowly. "If we were only in beef, we'd be broke. If it were only pork, we'd be better off. But instead, we got a double barrel of bad news."

Like many other farmers in this position, Langlois believes in the supply-management system for red meat. He has thought about it from many angles, and feels that this type of system represents a different attitude toward his fellow-farmers. "Many farmers think there is such a thing as free enterprise," he began. "So they oppose supply-management because of their fear of having their freedom controlled. But farmers have got to realise that we have limitations on our freedom, even to buy and sell. What we do affects everybody else, so when we act independently and competitively, we are not working co-operatively." Like many farmers, Langlois is upset about low market prices, but he doesn't think that government stabilisation plans will really solve the problem. He would like to see a fair price for red meat come from the marketplace, but he doesn't think that the marketplace always works well by itself. "The government should enter in when necessary to do justice where there is injustice," he added. "To allow these low market prices to continue is irresponsible. Farmers end up surviving at the expense of their equity. So they end up treating their farms as mines and not as renewable resources." Langlois talks as if he has had these thoughts on his mind for a long time. And he speaks from personal experience. Some of their own soil is suffering from water erosion because of their continuous cropping of corn, which they need to sell to keep the farm going. They'd like to rotate some of the land into a pasture crop such as alfalfa to help build up the soil, but with low meat prices, they can't afford to go a year without planting a cash crop. For them, that choice is a hard compromise. The Langlois family has strong religious beliefs about taking care of the soil and promoting social justice for farmers. Both John and Sue are active in a new farm group in southwestern Ontario called Catholic Rural Life. This organisation may be the only church-related one on record to support the controversial policy of supply-management for red meat;[3] for them, it is part of their belief that fair prices for farmers allow them to practice soil conservation which benefits both the land and society. John feels strongly that his economic views on farm issues belong in a larger moral context; in his case, that framework is the social teaching of the Catholic Church. "They've had hundreds of years of experience," he says. "They've been a leading influence over the years for justice in the workplace and they've developed a body of social doctrine that no one else has."

It's because he has such strong convictions that John is fairly perceptive about some of the stopgap solutions which many farmers are using to save their farms. For example, many younger people are finding it economically impossible to farm full-time, so they take second jobs off the farm. According to Statistics Canada, part-time farming is now practiced by as much as 35 percent of Canada's farm population;[4] both farm men and women often hold outside jobs to help finance the farm operation. But the idea of part-time farming just makes John Langlois angry. He once heard former federal agriculture minister Eugene Whalen comment that technological advances now allow farmers to take jobs off the farm. "If I could have hit him, I would have hit him," John said with annoyance. "Part-time farming is not the answer to our economic problems." He's not alone in his views. Many farmers are angered by the implication that agriculture in Canada can no longer sustain itself as a business. And farmers like John Langlois believe that without government policies and leadership, the most fundamental business in the country will turn into a part-time occupation for all but a wealthy few.

But John also found that subsidising the farm has another cruel twist. "For a while," he explains, "Sue had to work in both the farm and the house to keep the farm going. Five years ago, we realised that we had really misplaced our values, and that economics were forcing us to put our farm before the health of our family life. Our family was being sacrificed for the farm — and my wife and kids were being exploited." In his view, farm families make up with their unpaid labour for the relatively low prices the rest of us pay for food. (It should be mentioned that the hired man is no longer a fixture on many farms; the tight economy has put not just women, but also young kids to work manning tractors and other heavy farm machinery.) "The government is allowing the consuming public to feed off our equity while exploiting our kids and our wives, too," John remarked. It is a problem that we don't hear very much about; while some of us know that we get cheap fruit from Third World countries because labour is poorly paid, we forget that we get cheap food in Canada because most members of the farm family do the work for nothing. At this point, Sue spoke up. "I don't necessarily think we owe the consuming public an education," she said. "In fact, I don't really think they care and they won't care until the stuff is no longer on the supermarket shelves." She paused for a minute. "Maybe my attitude is just as bad as theirs," she said. But her annoyance with the consumer's failure to care about the farmer's plight has been echoed by almost every farmer I have ever met. Most of this annoyance centres on the feeling that consumers aren't paying a fair price for what they get; most farmers believe that government deliberately supports a "cheap food policy" to get election support in ridings dominated by urban voters.

But John Langlois also asks himself how far he is willing to go in order to challenge the injustices done to the farm community. He is one of the many farmers who believe that most farm organisations don't speak out strongly enough. "Being rational is not always effective," he said. "People don't pay attention if you talk nice all the time." John also knows that the Catholic Rural Life group will soon have to ask how blunt their approach should be in dealing with the farm economic crisis. "If you can identify an injustice," he asks, "to what extent do you feel you must right it? If there is an injustice, you may be obligated in conscience to be vocal and militant." But John freely admits that he is in a quandary about what he would actually do. While some farmers have engaged in direct confrontation with banks trying to foreclose, it is not likely that Langlois would get involved with this kind of activity. He plans to stay in farming and that will mean periodic visits to the bank and co-operation with his bank manager.

John and his family say they have learned a lot from their recent experience. They have cut back their operation and they plan to continue farming on a smaller scale. "We have to fight expansion," he says. "Smaller farms will provide better stewardship than larger ones." Some of his children want to farm and he hopes to leave them a healthy operation when they are old enough to take it over.

The situation this family faces is fairly typical: they expanded their operation and got caught in the squeeze of high interest rates and low farm prices. What makes them different is the way they try to understand their problems in a much larger context that involves the lives of many people beyond the farm gate. In this, they are almost unique. Most hard-pressed farmers feel under too much economic pressure to ask themselves whether farming ought to be a responsible way of living as well as a business.

Many people who are hurt by financial troubles try to continue life as normally as possible. But sometimes the strain shows through for both the farmer and his family. This is the case with Dan Pope, a bankrupt cattle producer, and one of Ontario's most outspoken farmers on the subject of changing beef marketing. He now lives about forty miles west of Hamilton, Ontario, on a quiet road just off Highway 52, past Peter's Corners. His house is a modest bungalow, built of red wood panels and gray stone. There were trees and flowerbeds around the house; some traces of farm life remained in view. Two bronze-coloured horses were grazing in the pasture next door. On the lawn, stood an old decorative farm wagon with a real estate "Open House" sign lying askew next to it. A broken baseball bat and bikes were lying in the driveway. Inside, the house was in disarray and two kids were staring at the TV. It was not until I talked to Dan that I understood the air of depression around the place.

Dan took me to the back yard; he made himself comfortable in his mother's old-fashioned wooden swing that rocked back and forth as he talked. His dog and cat chased each other around our feet during the conversation. The story he told is one of the most complicated I've ever heard and the elaborate arguments he has had with the banks are not easy to follow. But the basic outline of his story is fairly clear.

Dan was the youngest of six kids in a farm family, which had known hard times before. His dad was one of many who got started in farming in the 1920's, only to lose everything in the Depression. He began farming again in the Forties and in 1954 he sold his farm and bought two more. Dan took a two-year agriculture course at Guelph and he would have liked to study more, but there was no money. Meanwhile, his family's operation met a series of setbacks which Pope blames on their mistakes in following advice from the banks. They had been dairy farmers, before the milk marketing board was set up in the 1950's, and they expanded their operation when Dominion Dairies asked them to produce more milk for processing. Instead, the bank recommended that they get out of dairy and go into beef. That proved to be a costly mistake; shortly afterwards, milk came under the supply-management programme and dairy farmers found themselves receiving steady incomes.

There were more setbacks for the Popes; a poultry barn burned down in 1961 and when a second barn burned in 1963, they decided not to replace it. That also proved to be an expensive mistake; by the late Seventies, chicken, turkey and egg producers were all operating under supply-management which gave them some protection from the harsher blows of the farm recession. Pope ended up investing in the one area of farming that would be hurt most severely, and when I mentioned this to him, he said, "You do what you can do. When you talk to the banker, you find that money is there for this and not that... the Ontario Ministry of Agriculture was recommending specialisation, and we went along." In any case, the combination of the bank's advice, the recession and a series of errors put a stop to the business.

But the story doesn't end there. The house Dan lives in had been built on the original farm property; he had severed it off and moved in, and when his parents died, he moved back into the original farmhouse just over the hill. The sheriff removed them from the farm, which has since been sold. The bank could not seize his house as an asset because it was in his wife's name, while the farm itself was incorporated. His wife made an offer to buy the farm—and then found herself faced with a one and a half million dollar lawsuit from the bank. When I tried to sort out the logic of this, Pope simply said, "the message is 'you don't fool around with the bank.'" Later, the RCMP questioned one of the local businessmen about his dealings with Pope and when the dealer told Pope, he remarked, "Next time that happens, get that cop in the car and take him around with you to help you collect your outstanding accounts." Pope, like other militant farmers facing bankruptcy, is convinced that the police assist the banks when they lean on troublesome clients.

In spite of all these problems, Pope still wants to get his farm back, but he still faces costly lawyers' bills and more litigation. His experience has made him an angry man who distrusts banks and believes that most farmers do not realise the control they exercise over the way money is invested in food production. "There was good money in hogs in the early '70's," he explains. "But if a typical farmer wanted to expand, he'd be encouraged to build a big new specialised hog barn with a slatted floor. Even if the old-style barn would give the farmer more flexibility, farmers like to have the best—and after all," he added sarcastically, "banks couldn't conduct their farm tours if all they could show was old lean-tos added on to barns [for expansion]." Dan Pope—and many other farmers—say that banks have told them that they can only meet spiralling costs and high interest rates by specialising their operations. And because farmers caught in an economic vise are desperate for solutions, they are, in his words, "easily led" into more specialisation—which can often lead to higher costs in the long run.

From our vantage-point, it is hard to understand how some farmers can consistently take so much bad advice. And there is no doubt that some of them have made mistakes in business management. But it is also hard to understand how today's farmer can always be attentive to all the demands that are now placed upon his work. Along with the usual problems of trying to second-guess both the weather and the markets, the farmer now has to evaluate the ups and downs of labour costs, the behaviour of banks and multinationals, the effects of futures trade on markets and the whims of the consumer, not to mention how federal and provincial government policy toward agriculture is likely to affect his farm. Many farmers now feel that these trends are pushing agriculture into the hands of larger corporate interests. Farmers like Pope feel that this process is already under way, because of the influence that banks and multinationals have on farm operations. He described several cases in which banks insisted that farmers who were behind on their loan payments sell their grain immediately, even if it would have earned more money had they sold it later. He is angry that a bill which would have stopped farm foreclosures by setting up an arbitration procedure between banks and farmers died on the order paper just before the 1984 federal election. "Let me ask you a question," he said emphatically. "Who runs this country—the banks or the government? Who puts money into the till—the banks or the politicians?"

It comes as no surprise that Pope, like many other beef producers in his position, supports quotas and supply-management. He once sat on a committee of Ontario Cattle-men's Association members which met in order to pin down how such a plan might work. But the OCA executive, along with a narrow majority of its members, opposes the quota system. Knowing this makes Pope feel frustrated. "Just *how* terrible do things have to get before farmers organise?" he asked me angrily. It was a question I could not answer.

But farm debt and bankruptcy often have their most crushing effects upon the farm family's life. Financially, the Pope family is making ends meet with the income Dan earns in a trucking business and the money earned by his wife selling real estate. "The family has survived very well," Pope says, but that is only part of the truth. His wife suffered a nervous breakdown as a result of stress caused by the farm's problems; Dan feels that the chance to work has been good for her. The bankruptcy has also been hard on his kids in ways that count for younger people. Pope's fourteen-year-old son used to fix his bike in the shed that was part of the farm repossessed and sold by the bank; now he is unhappy that he can't go there anymore. That may sound like a minor detail to city people who are used to moving from place to place. But even today's younger farmers and their children have grown up with a strong sense of heritage and continuity, as their grandparents did. Often a farmer's land has belonged to the family—in some cases, for generations—and their values include a strong belief that at least one family member would be able to continue farming, if at all possible. This is an unspoken part of the farmer's mentality which only surfaces when the fabric of their rural existence starts to unravel. "I worry about my kids and how all this affects them," Dan mused, looking away as he spoke. "When I was a kid, I always knew where I was going. Now it's all different . . . we're not home together . . . we never eat as a family any-more," he added, a little sadly.

For people like Dan Pope, the economic crisis has dealt a blow not only to his livelihood, but to his family life—and beyond that, to the bond that is shared with the lifestyle of a larger rural community. While it is not always easy in such cases for the observer to sort out who was right and who was wrong, it is impossible to get away from the visible suffering

these problems cause everyone. But in spite of it all, Pope is
defiant. "You could never get a fellow [to sell] his farm if he
were able to make a living off it. We are willing to work
longer and harder for less money—as long as we have
enough. Still, I don't see what has happened to us as a
personal defeat. It's the country that failed us. We did our
best."

The town of Dunnville is on the south end of the Niagara
Peninsula, an area best known for its rich fruitland, good
soils and relatively mild climate. I was met at a farm by
Marjorie Ettinger, a dark-haired woman, nicely dressed in a
red shirt and blue slacks. Everything about the place seemed
in order, but I sensed immediately that something was not
quite right. Marjorie was not shy as she told me about the
financial difficulties her family has faced. But as she did so,
her eyes were wary and she scrutinized me carefully, never
taking her eyes off me as she spoke. Her story was one of an
old family farm that is now in trouble. It originally belonged
to her maternal great-grandfather and was passed down to
her grandfather. His daughter was Marjorie's mother and
his son (her uncle) was, in those days, the logical person to
inherit the farm. But there were problems between her uncle
and his dad; because of this, the man did not get title to the
farm until he was nearly too old to work it. At this point,
Marjorie's mother stepped in and bought the place, which
she later rented to her daughter and her son-in-law. The
Ettingers now own 90 acres of the farm and Marjorie's father
owns 200 acres; the two families farm together.

But for these fourth-generation farmers, things have not
gone smoothly. Marjorie's husband, Wayne, studied agriculture in Nova Scotia. When he joined the enterprise, he felt it
needed improvement, so they fixed the place up and made
some changes in the business. They had originally started
out as dairy farmers, but their operation wasn't big enough
to support them. They got a good mortgage from the Farm
Credit Corporation, the federal body which makes loans to
farmers for capital expenses. But their operation expenses
are high; almost all the cash they earn has to go to pay either
debts or high interest rates. They raise corn and barley. This

year they grew hay as a rotation crop so they could build up the soil which had been depleted from growing corn. Hay is not a big money-maker, and some of this year's hay couldn't be sold because it's too moist from all the rain. As a result, the Ettingers may have to purchase livestock to consume it.

Unlike other farm people I have met, Marjorie Ettinger takes these circumstances very personally; she feels badly about what is happening to her family farm. When she talks about providing necessities for herself and for her family, she is not quite sure if she is entitled to have them. "We did renovate and put some money into the house," she said. "But on a farm like this, if you spend on yourself, you feel guilty." She puts some income into the farm by working part-time at the post office; the rest of the time, her hands are full looking after the house and the family. One of her biggest concerns is the way her children feel about their lack of money. She explained to me that rural schools have become more centralised and farm children now meet city kids in the classroom. She believes that when her children see how prosperous some of their urban schoolmates are, they end up feeling second-class because they haven't got extra money to spend.

"Farmers *always* feel second-class, you know, going hat in hand to the bank. If your loan is called, you're out of business. The banker can pull the plug anytime he wants." Marjorie spoke about this with great intensity in her voice, and she never took her eyes off me. I could feel how angry she was. As she continued to talk, I found her scrutiny very disconcerting, almost a reproach. This feeling grew when she launched into a bitter attack on consumers and city people who don't understand the problems of the farmer. When I suggested that farm groups might network with urban interest groups to share their concerns, she said flatly that "urban people are not interested in organisations." This was a generalisation, and when I pointed that out, she commented, "Well, why should urban people understand? Do I care how Stelco makes steel? Why should they care how we make corn?" Her direct gaze almost turned into a glare.

My feeling that it was I who was being interviewed—and judged into the bargain—was unlike anything I had ever

experienced in dealing with farm people. It was so un-
nerving that finally I decided to get to the root of this problem
as tactfully as possible. I told Marjorie that I realised how
burdened she felt and I asked her if she had any friends off
the farm with whom she could talk about some of these
problems. Or, even better, maybe she could get together
with some other farm women from time to time as a support
group to help each other out. "I wouldn't talk about these
things to people," she said flatly. "I don't talk about my
problems to my friends. I'll talk to a stranger, but I wouldn't
tell these things to a friend." She emphasized the last word
and trained her eyes on me again. I got the point. She
continued, "You don't tell anyone how bad things are around
here. The bank is likely to find out you are in trouble." She
was right! I had forgotten how fast news travels in a small
town. But most of us would find it hard to carry a burden
like hers all alone.

What makes things worse is the fact that Marjorie is not at
all sure she will be able to hand down her family's farm to
her children, as it was handed down to her. And if the kids
decide to leave the farm, she doesn't know where they will
get the money to finance their education. Marjorie's oldest,
Karen, is a bright teenager who wants a different type of life,
away from the farm: for her, university is only a few years
away. Her ten-year-old brother, Don, loves the farm; he's a
round-faced tanned kid who grins proudly as he tells you
how he spends his time. He came out on the porch for a
while and he told me that he'd just finished haying the big
field across the road. He also runs the combine and drives
all three tractors—a fairly common set of chores for young
farm boys. If he is aware of the family's difficulties, he
doesn't show it. Instead, he told me that his classmates don't
know much about farming. "I tell them, 'our combine broke
down,' and they say, 'what's a combine?' And then," he said,
"I tell them 'a combine is a machine for harvesting grain.'"
He seemed happy knowing how to do these jobs that help
the family out. When he left, I told his mother I thought it
was good that he wanted to farm when he grew up. "Good?"
she asked sharply. "I don't know if it's good. It's not like

any other job, you know," she continued. "You live right in it. There's more emotion in it." She looked quickly out in the hay field and looked right at me again. "He may not be able to stay. And why should he?" She said that unhappily; I felt her bitterness, but also, her unspoken wish that he might stay.

After a while, we decided to go talk to her husband, Wayne. We walked down the driveway to the shed in back; there was a hay wagon sitting out front and bales of hay were piled up inside. Wayne was in the shed; he leaned up against the entrance while I sat on a bale and talked to him. He's a friendly man; his concerns were expressed more in terms of the familiar farm issues, rather than from the more personal perspective of his wife. Like many farmers, he has had some second thoughts about some of the policies of the provincial Ministry of Agriculture. He said officials have encouraged farmers to rent land and, in his words, "to milk it with soybeans and corn, causing erosion." And while he would like to use proper crop rotations, Wayne said this becomes very costly when there are payments to meet. He thinks there needs to be some more innovative planning by the Farm Credit Corporation to help out farmers who get hurt by low prices on the world market. Like many farmers, he's also critical of land speculation that has pushed the price of farmland far beyond the reach of farmers just starting in the business. "There are a lot of speculators in the Niagara Peninsula," he said. "City people with money to invest." He pointed out that while good land rents for about twenty dollars an acre in his area, the price can run as high as two hundred dollars an acre in nearby Kent and Essex counties. And since many farmers rent a few hundred acres of land a year, land rental can get very expensive.

Across the driveway from the shed, the Ettingers have a well-kept barn which they showed me. It was full of this summer's hay. As we walked down the slope from the barn to the driveway where I'd parked my car. Marjorie started to tell me a story that was on her mind. It was about a funeral she had been to the previous fall for a nearby farmer who was 101 years old. In all that time, he had lived on and farmed the same land and his children and their children had all farmed it after him. When he died, they buried him near the church, on a hill overlooking the home that had been his all his life. Marjorie stopped walking and stood in the driveway, looking at me as she spoke. "And that's the way farming is supposed to be," she said and she started to cry. "I wouldn't have talked about it if I knew I would be so emotional," she said. "But that's what it's all about. Farming is really a very emotional thing." She knew that well; if they were to lose her family's farm and home of four generations, a large part of her history would be torn away with it. Her grief was real, and all I could do was to tell her that I understood her feelings. I noticed that she had stopped staring at me. She even looked a bit relieved, and she was more relaxed and friendly by the time we said goodbye.

2
Wine and Milk

Ontario, along with British Columbia, has the most diversified farming in Canada. And farming in Ontario has dramatic
economic contrasts to match its variety of crops and livestock.
While many farmers face difficult times, the province also
has a number of prosperous and well-established farmers.
For these people, success has come for the same reasons as
it does to other business people who strike the right balance
among talent, good timing and luck. Many older, well-
established farmers bought land when prices were low, expanding their operations slowly and cautiously. While they
are highly mechanised, these farmers are very careful about
how they invest in state-of-the-art technology. Their approach
to capital expenses was summed up well by one wealthy
Quebec beef farmer who told me that "to be successful in
the business, you just don't run out and buy all the hardware
they tell you you have to have when you are in [agriculture]
school. You have to know when—if ever—to buy it. It's just
the same as knowing when to buy and sell your cattle." Most
important of all, many have done well because the times were

on their side and they were intelligent enough to turn good economic conditions to their own advantage. Not surprisingly, their sons and daughters who are taking over these prosperous farms are far less certain that they will have a future in the business.

For both generations, farming is a way of life as well as a way of earning a living. And with many older farmers, their interest in the family farm as an institution is a very real part of their concern for the future of their own businesses. This may explain why many of these well-established farmers speak with genuine sympathy about the problems of other farmers who are in financial trouble—a far cry from the more aggressively competitive attitude of urban business people. Farmers who make a good living usually feel a kinship with those who do not; whatever their incomes, both share in common a belief that society has little understanding of, or interest in their way of life.

Ontario's Niagara Peninsula is a two-hour drive from Toronto, going west on the QEW to the Port Colborne-Welland exit. The Vineland farming area is the centre of Ontario's grape production; if you drive along the back roads in early August, you can see rows of well-tended vines trailing against heavy wire, loaded with grapes which will soon be ready for harvest. From the Queen E, Route 24 runs south through the village of Vineland and over the curve of the Niagara Escarpment. A few turns down the road take you to an old white Ontario farmhouse, its lawn casually decorated with flowers and farm antiques. In back of the house is an open area and a large shed where farm machinery and a small plane are stored. Howard Staff came out to meet me, a cheerful man in work clothes, who took time out at a busy time of year to tell me about his farm operation. Staff told me that his family has been farming in the area for almost two hundred years, "since Butler's Rangers went to Queenston Heights to whump the Yanks!" The original farm had one hundred acres; they have been growing grapes for almost ninety years after farming cash crops and apples. They now own eleven hundred acres, a fairly large spread for Ontario, and each year they rent two to five hundred acres to grow some cash crops and vines. In addition to their own farm, they also manage some orchards for a Swiss investor.

Clearly, this is a big family business which has grown slowly over a very long period. Lots of hands keep it running smoothly: Staff and his two brothers employ fourteen people full-time and four to five hundred workers part-time each year. Grapes have been a big success for this farm business. Like many local growers, the Staffs began with some of the native Concord varieties which are processed into juice and jam; but they have since moved into the newer hybrid grapes which have helped to produce quality Ontario wines over the past few years. Howard Staff's awareness of this market reveals his good business skills; he explains that when farmers plant vines, they have to plan ahead ten years. In 1969, he had a "gut feeling" that he ought to plant white grapes for the wine market, even though the red varieties were selling better. "It was a move made on intuition," he says—and it paid off. Ten years later, white wine was in very high demand and growers were caught with stockpiles of surplus red grapes which the wineries didn't want.

The story of Niagara's grape surpluses involves more than changing tastes. All Ontario grape growers are facing surpluses because of a drop in wine sales and the Niagara grape business employs sixteen thousand people whose livelihood is threatened.[1] Grapes are a going concern for Niagara farmers; they now raise forty-five varieties, a fact that may surprise many Canadians who assume that Ontario grapes and wine are limited in type and quality. It was not very long ago that Ontario wine usually meant a product made from the native Labrusca grape—a sweeter variety better suited to juices and jams. Over the past fifteen years, researchers have developed hybrid varieties of the vinifera grapes used in the best European wines; these grapes can be grown in the unusually mild microclimate of the Peninsula. The European varieties are hardy in that warm pocket of southern Ontario and have gradually replaced the lower-quality varieties which were once the staple of Ontario's wineries. In recent years, several "cottage" wineries have opened in the area; their high-quality products make the dramatic improvement in Ontario wine hard to miss. The traditional wine-makers in the region have also improved their products, using the new hybrid grapes; their wines compare well in taste tests with European wines of the same type.[2]

Nevertheless, sales show that most Ontario residents are avoiding the local wines. Almost half of Ontario's population used to drink Niagara wines but in one year that number dropped to 38 percent. At the same time, the sales of imported French white wine jumped 66 percent, while sales of French red wine also rose 44 percent. In 1984, Ontario consumers drank over $224 million dollars' worth of the Ontario product,[3] but sales have suffered because of competition from cheap imports of good-quality wine. The problem began when the United States challenged an Ontario government handling charge of 65 cents a litre on imported wines, saying that the local "tariff" violated the terms of the General Agreement on Tariffs and Trade. Threatened with reprisals from the US, the Ontario government dropped the levy in 1983 and instead set a basic wholesale minimum price for all wine. Ontario's Liquor Control Board hoped that this manoeuvre would give a price advantage to Ontario's wines. But the pricing system gets more complicated: the LCBO also adds a mark-up of 123 percent for imported wines, plus the provincial sales tax of 12 percent—calculated on the cost of the wine after the federal excise duty and sales tax are added to it. While there is also a provincial tax on Ontario wines, the LCBO only marks them up by 58 percent. For the consumer, the elaborate calculations simply meant that the minimum price for many good Ontario wines would be in the four-dollar range, while the minimum price for a bottle of imported wine would be $5.60 a litre. Under the GATT rules, this was the largest price spread allowed between domestic and imported wine.[4]

Despite the price breaks, things have not worked out well for Ontario wineries. The carefully-constructed system fell apart when France devalued the franc. All at once, costly French wines became affordable because of the higher value of the Canadian dollar. Many good-quality imports cost little more than Ontario wines and consumers were willing to pay extra for the brandname imports.[5] That only added to the frustration of Ontario grape growers who already resented the farm subsidy policies of the European Economic Community. Farmers estimate that growers in the EEC are subsidised from 1.5 to 2 billion dollars a year; Howard Staff points out that "we can't compete against their pursestrings." Because government subsidies are so substantial, farmers in the EEC are encouraged to grow as many grapes as possible — with the result that Europe now has a seven hundred million gallon "sea of wine" which is being dumped on the North American market. To make matters worse, Niagara grape growers have had their own share of excellent crops. In 1984, they harvested 90 thousand tonnes of grapes, but the wineries only wanted 60 thousand tonnes.[6] As a result, the federal and provincial governments set up a cost-sharing programme to buy up fifteen million dollars' worth of Niagara grapes for processing and storing until the markets improve.[7]

In many ways, the problem of the grape grower is similar to the problems faced by all farmers who have to deal with competition from imports. Yet Ontario wine grapes are considered the most expensive in the world. Costs of energy, labour and bottling are higher here than in Europe, making our product a costly one. The wine industry hopes to overcome price resistance when and if the sale of wine in supermarkets is made legal in the province, which they believe would boost sales. Even so, local wineries have found it relatively difficult to get a good selection of Ontario wines into restaurants, where both owners and customers simply won't drink it.[8]

While the problems of grape growers are much like those of other farmers, solutions may be much more elusive. Ontario has a small but growing quality-wine industry, one which cannot compete on the world market without tariff protection. Is it legitimate for government to intervene to save a business which does not produce an essential food product? Certainly the labour-intensive grape and wine business creates jobs, not to mention tax revenue for both levels of government. That fact alone may insure that the industry is kept alive, although the recent federal budget increased the tax on alcoholic beverages, a hurtful move.

Despite these woes, production of other fruit on the Niagara
Peninsula has dropped over the past decade, and the amount
of land used for grape production has grown.[9] It is easy to
see why wealthy grape growers like Howard Staff may share
worries with farmers who are less well-off.

Another factor troubling the Peninsula is the growth
industry in absentee landlords. "Ten to fifteen percent of the
land around here is not owned by farmers," Howard Staff
explains. He spoke with annoyance about a deal made a few
years ago when southern Ontario's largest dairy farm was
bought by Italian investors. These speculators held on to the
property without looking after it; according to Staff, this
first-rate farm was reduced to "nothing but weeds." The land
is now rented out to local farmers for cash-cropping. When
Staff asked one European investor why he didn't look after
his local farmland, the man told him that it was better to
have his million dollars invested in Ontario land than to
keep it in Italy, where there was so much danger of political
unrest. "We don't appreciate that kind of thinking," Staff
said dryly.

In August 1984, there were about eleven hundred acres of
farmland for sale within three miles of Staff's farm, and he
had thoughts about expanding his operation. The family
buys small pieces of land when they feel the time is right;
Staff points out that "you need a land base to make a good
living." The cost of farmland is high, and it disturbs him to
see that many farmers have to work-part-time to pay off a
mortgage before they can get their farm business going. "It's
not real farming," he says adamantly. "A farmer should be
able to farm. And there are two kinds of family farm. Many
are farmed after dark, as long as Mom's back doesn't give out
and the kids don't leave home. And then there are the *real*
farmers who are really doing something." Not surprisingly,
he blames the growth of part-time farming on Ottawa's
cheap food policy. It bothers him that many farmers can no
longer make a living farming; what he finds just as annoying
is his awareness that many non-farmers resent the comforts
he feels he has worked hard to earn. "Why shouldn't I have a
good lifestyle, just like the guy at Ford or GM?" he asks.

"Grandfather put the barn up and father put up the implement shed," Staff told me, showing me around the place. "The family sticks together as a group; that's why we've got these things. It's not always easy; you are given your relatives, while you can choose your friends." He pointed out that most people who go into business expect to do well over a relatively short period of time. But when a family farm prospers, its wealth becomes part of the family's history of what its members have achieved together. Staff doesn't think that most city people understand this idea any more than they appreciate just how hard the farmer has to work. To prove his point, he told me an anecdote involving the manager of a local shoe store. One day, Staff noticed this man out in his vineyards, picking some grapes. He hadn't asked Staff for permission and, of course, had not offered to pay him for the fruit. Staff didn't try to stop him, but a few days later, he took his son to the man's shoe store. They selected a pair of shoes for the boy and then walked out of the store without paying for them — in front of the startled manager, who got the message.

Even wealthy farmers worry that Canada's agriculture could one day face a serious crisis if farm prices don't improve dramatically. At least dairy farmers — along with poultry and egg producers — are protected from sharp swings in prices through their supply-managed marketing board. While consumer groups worry that the system of milk quotas makes dairy products too expensive, farmers argue that the alternative to this marketing system is an unstable milk supply, rock-bottom prices and the gradual disappearance of Canada's milk business. They point out that before provincial marketing boards were set up in the 1960's, the market for milk and milk products in Canada was chaotic. Sometimes it was flooded with milk, while at other times, supplies were scarce. The farmer had no way of predicting the price he was going to get for shipping milk. No matter how large or small the supply, the farmer had no guarantee that he could sell what he produced. Farmers contracted their milk to processors who had the power to set both the price of milk and the volume they were willing to buy.

Under such uncertain market conditions, the industry got so disorganized that it became the subject of a major political debate. In 1963, officials in Ontario prepared a study which recommended that the dairy industry be completely reorganised.[10] The province passed legislation in 1965 permitting a farmer-run marketing board. Other provinces followed this example, and by 1970, Canada's dairy farmers had a national supply-management system. Provincial marketing boards now act as agents for the farmer, buying and selling his milk; processors have to negotiate a price on a yearly basis with their board.[11]

From a layman's point of view, the national dairy system is likely to look extremely complex and over-regulated. But it is a popular system and farmers seldom find fault with it. Part of its complexity has to do with the very nature of the milk business, since keeping supply and demand in balance across the country is not an easy task. Cows, of course, vary in the amounts of milk they give. And marketing boards also have the job of regulating thousands of small producers, rather than a few giant plants. The detailed milk quota system had to be designed to take these facts into account. In simple terms, a producer's quota represents his share in the market. Provincial boards operate two different types of quota systems; the first of these is completely regulated by the province and it controls the production of fluid (or table) milk. Because fresh table milk is in constant demand, farmers must produce their daily quota of fluid milk, issued in litres per day. This means that they have to fill as much of this daily quota as they can. Because of the effort involved in daily milk production, farmers who ship table milk under this quota system get the best prices.[12]

The provincial boards also administer the quota system for industrial milk — the milk used for dairy products such as butter, cheese and ice cream. It is known as Market-Sharing Quota (MSQ) because it covers the market across Canada; a farmer who holds MSQ fills a certain percentage of Canadian demand for the milk used in dairy products. Because these products are less perishable than fresh milk, farmers receive industrial-milk quota in litres per year; it has to be filled within the dairy year, which runs from August to July.[13]

The process of alloting quota starts with the Canadian Milk Supply-Management Committee, set up under the Canadian Dairy Commission, the body responsible for Canada's dairy policy. The Supply-Management Committee includes members of provincial marketing boards and representatives of each of the nine provincial governments (excluding Newfoundland) which have signed the national MSQ agreement. Officials from Agriculture Canada and other farm organisations also sit on the Committee as observers. The Committee is responsible for managing the national quota programme, making sure that supply stays in line with demand. When the Committee makes its yearly estimate of Canada's industrial milk needs, it divides up the total quota among the provinces according to a formula which is adjusted from time to time as provincial demands change. It is at this point that the provincial milk marketing board allots the yearly MSQ to its dairy farmers.[14] In effect, these yearly production decisions tell the farmer how to adjust the licence his quota gives him to produce for his slice of the milk market.

Meanwhile, the farmer who wants to buy quota, either to get into the dairy business or to expand his operation, has three options. He can buy quota from a member of his family since retiring parents will often sell their business to a son or daughter. Farmers who want to expand can buy milk quota if they purchase a complete dairy farm where the farm owner includes the quota as part of the price of the sale. In Ontario, most of the quota that changes hands goes through family members; however, most provinces also hold provincial auctions or quota exchanges as a third method of transferring quota.[15]

Provincial marketing boards buy and sell all the farmers' milk and they pay him according to several formulas. For fluid milk, the formula accounts for a farmer's costs of production and it includes a system of indexing for inflation. This formula is meant to be a pricing guide and not an absolute rule; if higher milk prices threaten to hurt the market, increases to the farmer can be modified or postponed. Under the national MSQ programme, farmers are paid by a formula which accounts for the costs of dairy farming across the country as well as the Consumer Price Index.[16] These are complicated pricing systems and because of their complexity, consumer groups have often questioned whether they are an accurate measure of the farmers' costs. But marketing boards insist that the farmer is being paid fairly and in line with inflation. They point out that between April 1975 and January 1984, there was a 72 percent increase in what farmers earned for dairy products, while the Consumer Price Index went up over 111 percent; within the CPI, over-all food costs rose 114 percent.[17]

This guaranteed monthly paycheque doesn't make farmers rich. All it does is give them some assurance that they will be able to operate within a stable industry that has a long-term future. Many producers argue that such an incentive is needed because their business is highly capital-intensive; farmers who may have to invest as much as half a million dollars in land, equipment and machinery might not want to do this unless they get a decent return on such a large investment. Whereas the board is supposed to cover farmers for their costs of production, even the most efficient farmers say that their rising costs can get well ahead of the pricing formula which their board adjusts from time to time.[18]

Fortunately, there are very few bankruptcies or foreclosures in dairy farming. But those farmers with outstanding success stories don't give all the credit to their milk board cheques. One of these farmers is Russ Rowntree, who is one of Canada's best-known dairy farmers and cattle breeders. His huge family operation, Rowntree Farms, sits north of Highway 401 and Derry Road on the outskirts of Toronto — the rural edge of a sprawling suburban area. The Rowntree name on the huge barn is visible from the road; you approach the farm by driving in a freshly-paved driveway, through a stone gate adjacent to their sprawling gray brick home. To the right is a swimming pool; the barn, silos and two other family homes sit further back on the property. It is a thoroughly modern streamlined operation. Unfortunately, all this impeccably groomed farmland — complete with prize-winning Holstein cattle — is surrounded by encroaching industrial development. Rowntree bought this farm in the 1960s. Two days after the purchase, Kodak bought two hundred acres on the southwest corner of the road. Kodak

has since built a plant there and other lots nearby are pep-
pered with signs advertising good sites for new industry.

Russ Rowntree is an older man who remembers days of
bleak poverty as he grew up and at first glance, Rowntree
doesn't quite fit into his plush surroundings. In spite of his
prosperity, he is the picture of an old-fashioned farmer in
coveralls, his ruddy face smiling at you from under an old
straw hat. Retired now, he helps out with the family business
run by his two sons. He is the third generation of his family
to farm in the area and credits his mother with his lifelong
fascination with dairy farming. He learned how to milk at
the age of six, and he has been in the dairy business ever
since. The Rowntrees have been milk producers for over
eighty years; they can recall a time when they once sold milk
in Toronto from a pushcart.

During the Second World War, he worked two farms
belonging to people who he says were "lured away" from
farming to work in high-paying defence-plant jobs in
Toronto. While he welcomed the chance to expand his
farming opportunities, this wartime experience made him
wary of what he sees as "government interference" in agriculture. Before the War, he explains, farms extended right
down to Eglinton Avenue, now a busy east-west thorough-
fare in the heart of Toronto. He feels that during the war
years, Ottawa made defence work in the city so lucrative that
many farmers could not resist. With men looking elsewhere
for a good income, Ottawa, in his view, further undermined
the farmer by pegging the price of food at fixed rates so that
England could import inexpensive food in wartime. With
low prices, the Canadian consumer also got the benefit.
"And that," Rowntree insists, "was the start of the Cheap
Food Policy."

After the war, his farming prospered; today, his family
owns five hundred acres of land and farms a total of one
thousand acres. Their herd of five to six hundred cows
includes seventy milking cows; the rest are used for breeding the top-producing Holsteins for which the Rowntrees
are known all over the world. When I asked him how he
became a top breeder, he just smiled and said, "I was always
inquisitive and I was a dreamer . . . that I could be as good as

the best." He took the time to learn about cattle breeding by talking to older farmers about their techniques; he later became one of the first directors of the local Maple Cattle Breeders' Co-op. His farm is now involved in the production and sale of cattle embryo transplants—a technology which takes multiple fertilized eggs from top quality cows and places them in surrogate cattle to produce a new generation of prize calves. The Rowntrees now sell embryo transplants to several countries; in 1983, they scored a coup by making the world's first embryo transplant sale to the Soviet Union to help that country start its own breeding programme.

Business success doesn't make this farm immune from troubles. Rowntree admits that it is only a matter of time before he will be forced to find another place to farm. There are eight thousand acres of industrially-zoned land in the immediate area and "you can't stop people with money from buying it." He is resigned to this industrial takeover; in fact, he even asked the nearby Brampton city council to put his farm in the industrial portion of their Official Plan. Rowntree explains that his creeks are getting polluted with chemicals that poison cattle. He recently lost two valuable animals that way, and one of them was carrying an embryo transplant. The road in front of his farm is about to be expanded into a four-lane highway. "I don't want to live on a street," he says. "I want to live on a road. Somebody's going to get killed." Like other farmers in the same situation, he knows he will no longer be able to take his slow-moving machinery out on the highway to get from one section of the farm to the next. Those expanded four lanes will no doubt help American Motors, which is building a plant nearby. There is a lot of public enthusiasm about job opportunities at that plant, while any hope of saving farmland in this area has been quietly given up. But Rowntree won't fight battles he feels he cannot win; he is prepared to concede that the farmland has been lost.

In many ways, Rowntree is an interesting combination of talented entrepreneur and old-time farmer. He is a strong supporter of the Federal Conservatives and their policy of closer ties with the US, pointing out that "we're sitting beside a giant. One-half of all US [farm]land can be double-cropped," he continued. "That's two hundred and fifty million acres! If we don't become all one country, we will need a lot of protection." While he himself often makes business deals with other prominent people, he still thinks and talks in many ways like a struggling farmer. During our interview, he often commented that "people with all the money have all the control"—an odd remark from a man whose hard work has helped him survive and prosper. It may be that even well-to-do farmers never feel completely secure; Rowntree sometimes spoke philosophically, as farmers do when they get used to crop losses and other disasters. "A farmer is always hopeful," he mused, looking off in the distance. "You learn from the weather." When I left, he was standing in his driveway, in the middle of all his prosperous land, still in his workclothes and old hat, a businessman who was, by instinct, also a farmer.

Older farmers who have been through the Depression often seem humane, philosophical people whose business success is touched with the knowledge of what hardship is all about. But the world of younger farmers is often very different. Take Larry Ness, a young dairy farmer whose Quebec family has been in the business for over a hundred years. Quebec, like Ontario, is a major milk producer in this country; it is worth mentioning that when we speak about the Canadian dairy business, we are most often referring to the situation in these two provinces. With two-thirds of Canada's population, Quebec and Ontario produce about 80 percent of all the milk we make into dairy products. They also supply about 75 percent of Canada's total demand for milk.[19]

The Ness family farms two hundred and fifty acres in Howick, about an hour's drive south of Montreal. Like Rowntree Farms, the family runs an embryo transplant programme; they breed Ayrshires, the brown and white patchy cows which give a rich, creamy milk. Larry is 28 years old, an enthusiastic farmer with alert hazel eyes, black hair and a big grin. He is the oldest in a family of four and like many younger farmers, he has had the benefit of an agricultural education. His family's farm has 170 head of cattle, including about fifty milk producers. What sets Larry apart from many other dairy farmers is his attitude toward the regulation of the milk industry. He is the only dairy farmer I have ever met who looks forward to the day when the supply-management system in dairy is abolished. According to him, the marketing board "evens things out. But," he adds, "for the long-term good, it is a bad thing." He believes that some producers who might not otherwise survive in the marketplace have been saved by a system which returns their production costs to them. As far as he is concerned, the free market system would regulate the supply of milk more efficiently than a system of quotas; he points to the US examples of the deregulation of airlines and the trucking industry which has cut prices so much that only the most efficient operators survive. He is especially critical of the costs of quota for young people who want to get into the dairy business.

When the Board started in the 1960's, farmers were simply given their quota, based on the amount of milk they had produced in the previous year.[20] Over time, quota began to acquire value as a capital asset. Larry Ness insists that "if a fellow wants to start a farm now [to buy] just what he needs, nothing extra, half of his total capital is involved in quota and the rest goes into land, buildings and machinery." Since quota is a farmer's share in the milk market, there has always been concern that young people could not get into the business, either because of the cost of quota or because there was not enough available. Provinces have tried to make sure all farmers have equal access to the sale of quota; in Quebec, farmers are legally allowed to buy and sell quota only through a regional auction sale held once a month. Quebec farmers are limited in the amount they can buy in order to reserve some for new dairy farmers. In Ontario, sales take place through a monthly quota exchange in which a computer establishes a price for available quota which agrees with the bids that buyers and sellers have placed on the exchange.[21]

Even some farmers who want supply-management don't like the idea that quota should have a value; the National Farmers' Union is in favour of free quota, while opponents of that idea point out that if farmers didn't have to pay for quota, there would be no way to decide which farmers were entitled to have the limited amount available. Larry Ness has no use for quotas at all. "I have three hundred thousand dollars worth of quota," he says. "That's six thousand a cow. But if you look around, you can get a cow for one thousand dollars." It is true that while the supply-management system protects farmers in a business where the supply of milk would otherwise get out of line with demand, it may not always be easy for beginning farmers to purchase the quota which the previous generation of farmers got for free. But many milk producers look at quota costs as just another business expense which has increased along with all the other costs of farming.

Marketing boards continue to insist that the value of a quota only represents what an individual producer is willing to pay to increase his share of the market as he works toward greater efficiency. To my knowledge, no one has ever studied whether the continued exchange of quota in this way invites speculation, as farmers who are anxious to expand inflate their bidding prices. But quota prices can also be pushed down by the complicated economics of the dairy industry. This apparently happened to many Ontario milk producers in 1974 when the cost of milking cows rose and the price of corn was high enough for farmers to sell it on the market rather than feed it to their cows. Both of these situations would prevent farmers from expanding in the dairy business, making the value of their quota "practically worthless" (in the words of one farm leader) for a period of time.[22]

The subject of quota values is a controversial one because of the widespread belief held by many consumer groups that the high costs of quota is added on to the price we pay for milk and milk products. According to the Milk Boards, the price farmers pay for their quota is not included in the formula which determines what they get paid for their milk. They maintain that the cost of quota comes out of the pockets of the farmers; they get no compensation for this capital expense.[23] In fact, it is worth noticing that a marketing-board increase of two or three cents for a kilo of butter or a litre of milk will be quickly matched by the milk processor and the retailer; the consumer, faced with a ten-cent increase in the price of butter or milk, is then told that the price jump is the farmer's fault. Marketing boards are, by law, obliged to open their books to the public; processors and retailers as private businesses do not have to answer for their pricing policies. Ontario and Quebec together hold about seventy-five percent of all the milk quota in the country. And both provinces insist that whatever the costs of quota, young farmers are still entering the business. According to the Ontario Milk Marketing Board's statistics, an average of about sixty new producers have joined the dairy business each year since the Quota Exchange was set up in 1980. In addition, about four hundred young farmers each year buy quota from their parents' operations to get started in farming on their own.[24]

While it is still controversial, the supply-management system is the one which most dairy farmers prefer; many of them believe that it is the only guarantee Canada has of a stable dairy industry in a country where the demand for milk and dairy products could otherwise never keep up with the supply. It is possible that supply-managed marketing boards are really a choice made on political grounds as well as economic ones; without quota and price protection, Canada might not have a dairy industry at all. With this system in place, farmers make Canada self-sufficient in dairy products, and they get good prices because they face restricted competition from imports. But Larry Ness is still not impressed. He explains that in the US, the total supply of milk is gradually going down as more farmers are squeezed out of the business; those who are still farming presumably get good prices. "If I had no roots, I'd go into dairy in the States," he comments.

Despite the system, even Quebec is losing milk producers. According to Larry Ness, Canada's top dairy province lost 600 milk producers between 1982 and 1983. There are now 18,000 dairy farmers in Quebec, but Larry says "there were 40,000 just a few years ago." In fact, many smaller dairy farms are going out of business; some of these are retiring farmers. The situation is similar in Ontario; a check of the monthly report from the Ontario Milk Marketing Board shows that while the amount of milk produced is going up, the actual number of producers has been gradually dropping. Between 1971 and 1981, there was a 47 percent drop in the number of dairy farmers, which went down from 26,000 to 14,000. But over that same decade, the amount of milk produced in Ontario went up six percent.[25]

It is not only the economic squeeze that is making farmers drop out. In many cases, farmers get out of dairy simply because it is one of the most demanding and time-consuming jobs in agriculture. Even today's mechanised dairy farmer has to be up at five a.m. to milk the cows—with no days off. "We work 365 days a week," one tired-looking dairy farmer told me. Realising her slip, she chuckled and said ruefully, "It just *feels* that way." It is not hard to understand why some of these hard-working people leave the business for urban jobs. Larry Ness has seen it happen in his own region. "Now if you look on that road from Richfield to the Brasserie in Howick," he explains, "my Dad can remember when there were thirteen dairy operations. I can remember eight. Now there are two left."

Ness combines some of the tough economic views of the New Right in the US with a belief in the importance of the small-scale family farm. In fact, he feels very strongly that a good dairy operation has to be family-run. "Some farmers can run theirs alone," he says, "and some need a hired man. But there are no really large dairy operations in Quebec. They are all family farms... and that is the only one that would survive. The large-sized farms come and go. On a dairy farm, you have to do everything absolutely right 365 days a year... and you can't if it's not family-run." The Ness family knows this to be a fact of life. They run a profitable farm business; they get one thousand litres of milk a day from their cows and they raise all their own cattle feed. They are also champion exhibitors; one of their cows was part of the Quebec herd that won first prize at the Wisconsin Dairy Expo in 1984. They also won an award at Toronto's Royal Winter Fair that same year. With this kind of success to back him up, it may not be surprising that Larry Ness believes so strongly that only the most efficient and productive farmers deserve to stay in business. He'd like to see these good farmers get more credit—but he'd give the money to the Farm Credit Corporation out of the federal funds in stabilisation programmes which subsidise the farm-gate price for certain commodities in a bad year. It is not a suggestion that would please too many farmers. Nevertheless, his free-enterprise approach sets him apart as a younger farmer who has profited from the regulation of the dairy industry without being aware that its complicated rules and pricing system are there to solve a problem he has never experienced. Many other younger farmers who have no control over the prices they get might envy his situation.

It is clear that anyone looking for the farm crisis in the vicinity of most dairy farms will have to look further. Ness and Rowntree belong to well-established farm families which have invested huge sums of money in their businesses. There is not much chance that they will go broke. Certainly, these are not the farmers we hear about in the headlines. Agriculture still means good business for those who got started at the right time. Whether it will continue to be for their children is another matter. All of these farmers buy a high-powered view of success; they believe that those who make it must have the capital and business acumen to manage a complex farm industry. Not everyone wants to farm that way and many young people cannot afford it. But if we see farming as a mass-production industry, only those with generations of wealth and financial clout will be able to survive and prosper.

Farmers protected by marketing boards reap the benefits of a federal policy which makes Canada as self-sufficient as possible in milk, eggs and poultry. Without this protection, many of them might not exist. Fair or not, the boards give these farmers a living and the rest of us a steady supply of their products. Farmers will have to decide if supply-managed marketing boards are an answer to their economic problems. In the meantime, farmers fortunate enough to hold quota or inherit the family farm have a big head start in the business of survival.

3
The Grain Belt

Farmers in Saskatchewan, both rich and less so, face many of the same difficulties as their eastern counterparts, but they do not always share the uneasy mood. On the Prairies, people act as if they should take hard times for granted, and many treat economic woes as a recurring nuisance, like grasshoppers or a prairie blizzard. In some ways, this attitude seems to help these hard-pressed farmers for some of them have become more adept at dealing with their problems than many of their eastern counterparts less used to adversity.

Farming is the mainstay of Saskatchewan's economy and farmers often work the same land their families settled in the early part of this century. To an outsider, Saskatchewan feels like pioneer country and rural life has pleasing informality. As a stranger to the Prairies, I benefitted from the fabled hospitality as I tried to find my way through the maze of dusty back roads that crisscross the plains south of Regina. Unlike the meticulous labelling on country roads in Ontario and Quebec, Saskatchewan roads rely on the driver's sense of direction and familiarity with local landmarks. To an outsider, one expanse of flatness looks just like any other. Fortunately, I was often stopped by an observant farmer who could easily spot the look of the lost, and people routinely pulled their trucks over to help out. Farmers here have had to learn friendly co-operation to live in a landscape as stark as the prairies. Brown and cream-coloured stubble in the autumn fields spread out flat in every direction, catching an eerie morning light filtered through clouds. Along the side of the road, the scattered barns, houses, granaries and elevators looked tiny and inconsequential under the huge blue sky, minor additions to a massive natural landscape. If farmers feel small too, they do not talk about it, but their feeling of resignation is sometimes hard to miss.

The town of Sedley is just about a forty-minute drive southwest of Regina on Highway 33. Typical of many small prairie communities, it sits adjacent to the railway tracks and grain elevators on the north side of the road. Across the way is the local seed-cleaning plant, an odd structure with spidery pipes and poles jutting out like tentacles. In the middle of town stand several small shops, including a credit union and a few clusters of houses huddled together. About five miles further down the road, I found a small white farmhouse, a shed and a big red barn with the name "Muxlow" on it. I pulled my car up in front of the house and went over to meet Doreen Muxlow who was out near the shed. She is a cheerful, middle-aged woman wearing sunglasses and a bandana around her light-brown curly hair. Before I came, she had been at work butchering and cleaning some of the three hundred chickens they raise on the farm. Her place is average in size for the area—about two sections, or twelve hundred and eighty acres. (A section equals one square mile, or six hundred and forty acres). Most of it is used for growing grain; a small amount of it is pasture land. But in one respect, this is not a typical farm. Doreen and her two daughters are its sole proprietors; four and a half years ago, Doreen's husband was killed in an accident. She and her daughters now do all the heavy farm work; they also make the management decisions—which include budgeting for major expenses such as their recent purchase of a new $95,000 tractor. They are frugal people; this purchase was a necessity for a farm where almost all the land and all the buildings and machinery are owned outright without any loans or mortgages.

Doreen took me into her house and we walked into the kitchen, where the floor was covered with newspapers and freshly plucked and slaughtered chickens. Doreen's mother was there to help with the work; she is over eighty, but looks much younger. We walked into an L-shaped living-dining room crammed full of things—furniture, a dining room table, a piano, pictures, bric-a-brac. Doreen was a bit apologetic about the way things looked, but like any farmhouse at harvest time, the indoor chores get neglected because of the demands of the work that has to get done outside.

While we had tea, Doreen told me more about her farm operation. She owns all her land except for one-half section; they grow wheat and a little barley and oats for her daughter's horses. Besides chickens, they raise fifty turkeys and fifty pheasants. Her farm has been in the family since 1905, when Saskatchewan settlers received homesteads from the Crown. Her dad farmed three quarter-sections and he gave one each to her and to her two sisters. She and her two daughters are very attached to the place; "it's ours to be proud of," she says. Her oldest daughter, Joan, 21, works full-time on the farm. She walked in as we were talking, a slim fair-haired girl with a striped jersey, jeans and work boots. Her mother had been telling me that Joan wanted to work on the farm permanently and that she didn't like the city job she had once held. As she walked across the room, her mother stopped her. "Tell me," she asked her daughter, "if anything happened to Mom, would you still farm this place?" "Oh, yeah," Joan answered casually, as if she were agreeing to run an errand. Doreen explained that Joan also keeps some livestock of her own from her father's estate, including a cow that produces calves that are sold for beef. Joan's younger sister, Laura, who is eighteen, works at the credit union, but she also does a lot of the farm work, which includes combining the grain at harvest time.

The Muxlows are realists, for, in fact, farmers in this province have had more than their share of worries. In the summer of 1984, the southern third of Saskatchewan, Alberta and Manitoba was hit with the worst drought in sixty-five years. Some areas went for seven weeks without rain; farmers lost twenty-five percent of their crops, which cost them about one and a half billion dollars in lost revenue.[1] As if that weren't bad enough, the hot, dry weather proved perfect for grasshoppers which showed up in droves to mow down what was left of the crop. The grasshoppers returned in the summer of 1985, hitting the Prairies with the worst infestation in fifty years. The drought that summer was so severe that many farmers stopped trying to control the pests with insecticides since many crops were too small to bother protecting. No one knows for sure if the Prairie dry spell of the past two years is the beginning of a longer cycle of drought that could last years.[2] Farmers who know about the Dust Bowl of the 1930's are doing more now to prevent their dry topsoil from blowing away in dust storms, and today use better conservation measures. The occasional clumps of trees you see as you drive across the prairie have been put there to prevent the dry soil from blowing away in a high wind. The only compensation for this drought is a financial one; farmers are entitled to receive assistance in the form of payments under a federal plan to which they contribute. Many of them need this money to buy seed for spring planting which they could not otherwise afford.[3]

Doreen Muxlow lives in the kind of community where neighbours still go out of their way to help each other. The day after her husband's funeral, twenty local men came onto her land and seeded her entire crop in one day. "Now that's community," she says. She herself is involved in a number of local activities in addition to her farm chores. And while she was hit by the recent drought, she was still able to harvest more grain than she expected. "You can always look to next year," Doreen remarks. "I've always looked forward to spring, I'm a gambler and farming is the biggest gamble there is." Like all farmers across the country, she is caught between the high costs of running a farm and the low prices she gets for her crops. But while she is able to live within her means, she is worried about young people who are having a hard time getting started in farming. And like many other western farmers, she is concerned about soil erosion. Some of her land has been damaged, quite possibly by a common prairie farming technique used here to keep the moisture in the soil. Because prairie farmers get relatively little rain, they leave part of their land unplanted each year so that the crop stubble left on the ground can hold the moisture in the soil that accumulates from rain and snow. According to a recent Senate report, there is evidence that this practice, known as summerfallowing, has actually caused soil damage; over time, the moisture in the crop residues finds its way down into the subsoils where it dissolves salts deep in the ground and brings them up to the surface. Nothing can grow on these saline soils which are becoming more widespread across the Prairies.[4] Doreen has a corner of one section in this condition. But every year, she summerfallows half her land, explaining that she has little choice because summer-fallow also gives the land a rest. If that's not done, she would have to grow grain year after year, running up huge bills for seed and chemicals. "And I'm not convinced that chemicals are doing anything for the soil," Doreen says.

While other farmers may feel that consumers get cheap food at their expense, Doreen is sympathetic to the problems of city people. She knows that the two groups often mis-understand each other and "live in two different worlds," but she feels that consumers are having just as hard a time financially as farmers are. And while people like herself get some assistance from government, she worries about how far that help ought to go. Like most farmers I talked to, she would like to remain as economically self-sufficient as possible. "My husband used to say, 'if your plate is full, why do you want more?' " she concluded.

Turning back north on the town road, I arrived at a tidy white frame house belonging to Peter and Yvette Warnke. Peter explained that his family came to Saskatchewan as homesteaders in 1902; he has been farming for 22 years. He owns seven hundred acres and rents another four hundred. While raising grain is his main source of income, he has joined the growing number of farmers who no longer make a full-time living from the land. To help meet his financial obligations, he works part-time as an electrician in the area. He points out that the interest on his loans is his biggest expense; he has mortgages to pay on some of his land, and like many other farmers, he has an operating line of credit with the bank when he needs to borrow money to start planting in spring. But he also adds that he sat on the board of the local credit union for nine years, and in that time, the financial situation of local farmers has not changed drastically. Still, the cost of machinery and repairs are up; last year, he had to pay out eight to ten thousand dollars for machinery and parts. That was a bad year; usually, his bill is much lower than that.

Last year, he sold a quarter-section of land to ease his finances. His second biggest expense is for fertilizer and chemicals, which is why he summerfallows a third of his land each year. While he's not convinced that summerfallowing makes the land saline, he says he has one hundred acres with an "alkali" (salt) problem. Yvette laughed when he mentioned this. "Nothing grows there but old vehicles," she chuckled. What really worries Peter is the expense of fertilizer, and how much he needs to use. Over the years, he's had to increase the amounts he puts on the soil in order to keep getting his usual crop yields. He puts about sixty pounds of nitrogen fertilizer on every acre he farms. He points out that he can no longer get the usual good yield of 30 to 35 bushels per acre. He explains that some farmers in Europe now have to put as much as three to five hundred pounds of fertilizer on each acre of soil to get any crops at all.

Peter Warnke's observations of what has happened on his farm are confirmed by the recent Senate Soil Erosion Report, which points out that the fertility of prairie soils has been decreasing over the years. According to the report, these soils were naturally fertile when they were first worked in the late 19th century by farmers who needed to use very little chemical fertilizer to get a good crop. But the report adds that the crop residues from summerfallowing that go back into the soil contain less rich organic matter than the original grasses that made up the fertile virgin land of the

Prairies. Over time, the soil has lost its original high carbon content; intensive farm production has also helped to deplete the soil of its nutrients. Soils which once produced 125 pounds of nitrogen per acre without adding fertilizer now release as little as nine or ten pounds of nitrogen per acre, if no fertilizer is added.[5]

This is only one of the farm issues which Peter has looked at from his vantage-point as a board member of a durable Prairie instituion: the Saskatchewan Wheat Pool. The Pool is a farmer-owned and controlled co-op; with seventy thousand members, it is one of the largest co-ops in Canada, as well as one of the largest grain-handling organizations in the country. It was started by farmers in 1924 to bargain for better grain prices. This role has since been taken over by the Canadian Wheat Board, the federal agency which is responsible for all sales of Canadian wheat, oats and barley on the world market.[6] That market for Canadian grain has expanded over the past few years; ever since the US grain embargo of the Soviet Union, that country has looked to Canada as a more reliable grain supplier, increasing its orders and cutting into the US grain market. Canada's grain sales have also been boosted by the fact that we, unlike the US have a national agency that can enter into long-term contracts with other importing agencies in the Soviet Union and China.[7]

Even so, many Canadians are not aware that the farmers who live in these isolated hamlets scattered across the Prairies are the producers of Canada's largest single export. Grain accounts for six billion dollars' worth of Canada's eighteen-billion dollar export market. Three-quarters of that grain is wheat.[8] Farmers are paid for their grain through the Wheat Board, which sells the grain and makes an initial payment to farmers at the time that the product is delivered to customers. Later in the crop year, farmers get interim and final payments based on the proceeds of the grain sales after handling charges and other costs have been deducted. While farmers know they can't control the fluctuations of the world grain market, almost all of them are satisfied with the Wheat Board's performance as a sales agent for their grain. The issue that has really disturbed western farmers—to the point of breaking up several prairie farm group coalitions—can be summed up in two syllables: the Crow.

The old statutory Crow's Nest Pass freight rates for shipping grain were abolished by Parliament in 1984 and replaced with a system which charges the farmer the cost of getting the grain to port. What seems like a straightforward and rather dull issue to many Canadians turns out to be a complex and emotional problem to many westerners—one by which some of them measure the place of the West in Canada as a whole. Those who wanted to save the Crow saw it as a promise that was made to the West by Ottawa to allow it to enter Confederation on an equal footing with the more prosperous eastern half of the country. The agreement on a fixed grain shipping rate was made between the federal government and the Canadian Pacific Railway in 1887. It came about because the CPR wanted to put a route through the mineral-rich area of southeastern British Columbia. The federal government was happy to strike a bargain with CPR because of fears that the Americans might move into the area if Canada did not develop it quickly. Ottawa gave CPR a grant of almost three and a half million dollars—a sizable sum in 1897—and the B.C. government made a land grant to the railway of close to four million acres. In return CPR promised to ship grain at a fixed rate "in perpetuity" and the promise was formalized as legislation in Parliament twenty years later.[9]

But in recent years, the CPR insisted that it was losing money transporting grain; it cost less to ship a bushel of grain to Canadian ports than it did to mail a first-class letter. Other commodity groups shipping minerals and other products by rail complained of discrimination. And CPR said that the financial drain of the Crow rate left it without the funds to upgrade its rail lines or to add new cars to the system.[10] Many farmers accepted these arguments, in the hope that a more up-to-date railway would get their grain to market faster and put more money in their pockets. But an equally large number of farmers disagreed. They held that the CPR got more than its money's worth from federal funding and the B.C. land grant received in exchange for the low rate; they believed that the nationwide holdings the CPR built up over the years more than compensates them for any loss they took shipping grain.

Wayne Easter, president of the National Farmers' Union, agrees with this view. "Nothing will change the face of agriculture more than the changes to the Crow Statute," he maintains. "Only the low rates get talked about. What about the benefits the railway got? CP developed a huge empire in western, central and eastern Canada."[11] Easter explains that Canada's grain economy involves a huge export market. But he adds that in order to come to terms with such a grain-based economy in the most effective way, we have to recognise our geographical handicaps. In Canada, grain has to be moved over the Rockies or across the Great Lakes in order to get to export terminals; in the United States, grain is more easily shipped across the plains and down the Mississippi River. Easter believes that if transport costs keep going up, the price of Canadian grain will have to drop in order to be competitive on the world market.

Most farmers favoured the Crow because they were afraid of being hit with a big bill for grain shipping costs — especially during an economic slump. In spite of their concerns, the Crow was abolished and farmers can now pay up to $5,000 a year to ship their grain to port. Because there will be annual increases in that rate, some farmers could pay as much as $25,000 a year by 1991. During his federal election campaign, Brian Mulroney urged Ottawa to freeze a new increase in freight rates because the prairie drought had hurt farmers' incomes.[12] But since he took office, there's been no change in the freight rate policy. Peter Warnke says that he, for one, is cynical about the federal government and he doesn't expect any favours since "the CPR controls enough of government."

Warnke and most other prairie farmers are now resigned to the Crow change. He told me that many farmers in the area are now trying out new varieties of unusual crops which might earn them a little more money. This year, Warnke planted one hundred acres of winter wheat, the soft wheat used in pastry flour usually planted in eastern Canada. He and other farmers have been trying out a new strain that tolerates the harsh weather on the Prairies. Winter wheat has another benefit; it is planted in the fall and when it starts growing in spring, it competes with the wild oats which are usually a nuisance in the standard "hard" wheat crop, which is planted later. Since winter wheat is harvested earlier than hard spring wheat, the two crops don't compete with each other. About half the farmers in the Sedley area are planting some soft wheat; others are trying out legume crops such as lentils or chickpeas. There are foreign markets for these products, and they do not have to be sold through the Wheat Board.

Here, as elsewhere, good farmland is rapidly disappearing. While the prairie lands look vast Warnke points out that in the last ten years, the city of Regina has gradually spread out housing developments on good farmland. He wonders how young people will be able to get into farming if the price of land keeps going up. When I asked him why he stayed in farming, he paused and then he just laughed out loud. "I can't answer!," he chuckled. But then, he thought a minute. "My house is paid for," he said, "and it's a way of life, I guess, an investment in the future. You invest in it all your life . . . and we stay because we like it. I like sitting on a tractor—I can daydream—and it allows me time to be a mechanic, too . . . farming is a way of life more than a business. Or else, ninety-five percent of farmers wouldn't be in it."

Just outside the northwest corner of Moose Jaw, Saskatchewan, stands a brand-new suburban housing development on the edge of a flat open field that once belonged to a farm. The corner house on Daisy Crescent lives up to the name of the street: a cheery split-level house, bright yellow with white trim. It belongs to Ray and Irene Smith, a semi-retired couple whose farm a short drive away is managed by their son, Lorne. Smith has been farming since he was eighteen years old, and the signs of his success are all around his beautiful home. Our conversation is interrupted once by a call from his son at the farm, who chats with his dad by a C.B. hookup. The Smiths belong to a generation of people who have not forgotten the hardships of farming during the Depression and, with some justification, they believe they have earned the rewards of their hard work and perseverance. The family farms seven quarter-sections of land, all adjacent to each other. The original "home quarter" has been farmed by Smith's family since the early part of the century; he bought all the rest of the land himself.

The problems of the farm economy in this part of the country are complicated by loss of farmland because of soil erosion and the expansion of Moose Jaw. The area south of the Smith farm has had one of the most severe erosion problems in the country; a small portion of their own land has been affected, too. "We can't afford to carry out procedures to save our land," Ray says. "We had a very mild winter [in 1984] and no snow." One part of his land is half-summerfallowed each year and he uses no fertilizers or sprays on it. He summerfallows two-thirds of another chunk of land each year; the planted areas here are treated with chemicals. "It's a costly practice," Smith admits. "And we don't know if the long-range effect [of chemicals] is good or not." Not only is soil erosion a problem, but he sees land development swallowing up nearby farmland. Ten years ago, he explains, land sold for $150 an acre. But over the past five years, that same land has been selling from $700 to $1,000 an acre, from both speculation and inflation.

The Smiths' concern for farmland was evident when they took me for a drive on the back roads to visit their farm. As we drove over the flat prairie, they pointed out particular farms along the way. We passed one huge spread and Ray said, "City people own this. They just want a living from it, but they don't have a feel for it." He adds that many farms in the area range in size from one-half to three-quarters of a section. That is a manageable size; above two sections, he adds, you have to hire help. Originally, homesteads in the area were a quarter-section each. While today's farmer often owns a larger spread, the Smiths acknowledge that some farmers have really gone too far. "There's one guy around here who's on a real ego-trip," said Ray, a little glumly. "He's going for thirty-six sections of land. He likes to run around saying, 'I want to buy a township,' because that's what thirty-six sections of land is."

We came to their farm and drove into the laneway; next to a small grove of evergreens. At the end of the drive is a barn with "Sunnyside Farm" printed on it in big letters. His son Lorne lives there; he was outside near the barn with his little boy Jason, who was riding around on his bike. They explained to me that they have no pasture land; the soil is too good for grazing cattle and there simply isn't enough water. But they have obviously done very well as a grain operation; the outbuildings and grounds were quite impressive.

After my tour of the farm, I was invited into the kitchen to visit with the family and to talk with Ray and Lorne about how they see the future of their operation. Because Ray has done well at farming, I asked him what it was that has made him a success. He thought about it a moment and then said, "Caution. Hard work. Not going with trends too much. Dad set up this place well for me to carry on. We're in good land — some of the best in North America." Ray's farm grew and prospered at a time when the economy was faring better than it is today; his son Lorne no doubt knows this, and wonders if he'll be able to make it. "My income is dropping steadily. Cash flow is zilch. I have four friends around here who have packed it in," he said tersely. "We have no control over our prices," he continued. "The Japanese government buys wheat for seven dollars a bushel and then it sells it to millers for $35. If the price of grain went up with inflation, then we would get twelve to thirteen dollars a bushel." He had a point. The prairie farmer has been getting about four dollars a bushel for grain for the past ten years.

People like Lorne find themselves in a situation that must be very trying, both economically and personally. For young people who have inherited a very successful farm from hard-working parents, there is a real fear that they could lose their farm business and with it, the labour of several generations. With the high costs of energy, farm machinery and chemicals, the operation of such a big farm has become prohibitively expensive. Lorne is hardly the first young farmer I have ever met who is afraid his generation will be the last one on the land. His parents are quietly supportive; they know he is finding it tough. Over lunch, Irene said to me, "I know he's discouraged; I don't want him to feel that way, but at the same time, I want him to realise that farming isn't all rosy."

I decided to stop by the Swenson farm while I was south of Moose Jaw because I wanted to talk to people who were trying to tackle the problem of soil erosion. That's how I met Don Swenson and his son Richard who farm together about twelve miles southeast of Moose Jaw. When I got to their place, I realised I had come to an unusual farm; not only have they prospered here, but their work on irrigation and land reclamation draws visitors from all over the world.

Don and Richard have a partnership and they farm two sections of land; the Swenson family has farmed in the area since 1935. Don's dad was a Swede from the US who had seven sons. He bought a quarter-section of land and the house that sat on it for $500. But only ten acres of it were arable, and eventually, he paid another $500 for another half-section of land. Don started farming in 1945, adding on another quarter-section for which he paid $400. But none of the land was very good for farming and a lot of Don's effort over the years has gone into developing methods for soil reclamation and irrigation. The Swensons are now involved with nine other farm families in a new project which Don started: making fertilizer from the phosphates and nitrogen found in the Regina-Moose Jaw water supply.

I felt I had come to a wealthy farm, but I soon found that its owners are not pleased with their economic situation. Don explained, "We've faced adversity, but we're still here. It makes you more conscious . . . so you don't expand too fast. But two years ago, grain prices jumped. Then they were hit. That kind of thing makes it tough for young people. We have no price protection." Like many other farmers, he wants to see an effective system developed to get his grain to market faster, but he's worried about the escalation of shipping rates since the abolition of the Crow. "What degree of responsibility do the railroads have?" Don asks. "Are we paying for it in the price [we pay for] coal and oil?" He has an interesting solution for the problem of shipping costs: he would like to see the federal government own the roadbeds, just as it now owns roads and airports. If this were the case, Ottawa could license carriers who use the rails and commodity groups could purchase their own hopper cars for shipping grain, offering some competition to the railroads.

Don's son, Richard Swenson is an active Progressive Conservative; he headed Saskatchewan's federal PC election campaign in 1980. He studied Political Science and history at university and this background gives him a larger context in which to view the problems of his business. But what he had to say about it would not please many people, especially eastern Canadians. "We are being exploited," Richard says firmly. "People here who have tried to diversify have found that their closest processing plants are in Alberta. And the federal government ends up protecting the [eastern processing] sector that doesn't really need it. We want to be able to grow things that are good for our land and to make a decent living. We need a fair price system—period. Let's get rid of the protective tariff system," he said angrily, "especially for those one-hundred-year-old infants down East. We in the West have to sell on this protected world market. And I haven't got a crack at the eastern market [with my grain] because of their canola and soybeans." His frustration spilled over to other sectors of the family enterprise. "I sell cattle on the hoof and I can't afford to feed it." And he added sarcastically, "Thank God half the world is communist and can't feed themselves."

Like many big farmers in this area, Richard belongs to several commodity groups, but he feels that western farm organisations are too busy competing with each other to make their voices heard in the East. Richard looks to the US as a good example for farm groups to follow; he explains that in Washington DC, agriculture lobbyists spend millions of dollars to educate the public about farm problems. Here, he said with annoyance, farmers have received five hundred million dollars under a Wheat Board stabilization programme to compensate them for rock-bottom wheat prices over several years. "So," he added with disgust, "the headlines just read 'Farmers Get Five Hundred Million.'"

To my surprise, I did not sense acute crisis as I spoke to farmers in Saskatchewan in the summer of 1984. Today's drought conditions recall the Dust Bowl of the Thirties;

because they cannot be changed, some farmers have resigned themselves to a way of life which includes these hardships. On the other hand, Saskatchewan has its wealthy farmers who play for large stakes in the highly competitive world of international agribusiness. From their fortunate perspective, profits are shrinking, but these are hardly farmers on the verge of bankruptcy. Saskatchewan has its share of farm failures, but it also has regulated prices and a solid world market for its Number One crop. While Wheat Board payments do not make farmers rich, they protect them from extreme price fluctuations. Whatever its shortcomings, the Wheat Board was the successful end result of farmers' demand for fair prices during the depression. Having learned the rudiments of co-operative marketing, Saskatchewan farmers have an advantage over many in Ontario who are also feeling the pinch.

Nevertheless, there is a farm disaster looming in Saskatchewan, one broader than the economic concerns of the individual farmer. Two summers of drought combined with severe topsoil erosion are hurting farmland as well as the farm economy. Some of these problems point straight to the mixed blessing of a single cash crop. Western farmers are caught in a bind. If they grow only wheat year after year, they deplete the soil; if they rest the soil by summer-fallowing, they erode it. Meanwhile, a grain-based economy keeps the Saskatchewan farmer in business—for now. Perhaps it is fair to say that the real farm crisis on the Prairies is an ecological one; the farmers are managing, but the land is in dire peril.

4
B.C. Fruit Growers

As the tourist brochures insist, British Columbia is different. While farmers here raise the same crops and livestock as in Ontario or Quebec, no other farming region in Canada enjoys B.C.'s mild coastal climate or the combination of dry, clear weather and fertile soils found in the interior. The land itself is intensively cultivated, but many farm regions are surrounded by spectacular views of the peaks, forest or desert, a rugged environment in contrast to the modest scale of many farms.

The Okanagan Valley in the south-eastern part of the province is full of small, intensively-farmed orchards, a remarkable fact when you realise that the area is a desert which receives only about eight inches of rainfall a year. The fertile soil is well-irrigated, producing lush orchards in the valley that spans both sides of the Okanagan River. The route into the valley driving east along Highway 3 is one that a newcomer drives with care, with many sheer drops and jarring hairpin turns. I drove into Osooyoos, a small town about a mile or two from the Washington State border. Not far from the centre of town, there is a farm belonging to George Fraser, a local fruit grower whose family came to farm in the Okanagan shortly after the First World War, when it became involved with a group of people who formed a company to buy and sell land. It was evening when we sat down to talk in his kitchen. During the harvest period, days are usually too busy for farmers to stop and talk.

By now, I was prepared to hear the familiar story of the economic squeeze and how it affected this particular farm. I wasn't disappointed. But I also found that farm politics have worked in the farmer's favour in this area where many farms do not fit the norm. For example, Fraser told me that he farmed forty acres, a tiny operation by western standards. But he explained that ninety percent of the farms in the Okanagan are smaller; when the area was first settled, the land was parcelled out in ten-acre lots, a size which was once enough to support a family farm. While those lots are now too small to make money, the cost of farmland is high and farmers who can't afford to buy more land have to cultivate what land they have very intensively. "You're stuck with what you've got," Fraser said matter-of-factly. In this part of the valley, all the land that can be cultivated is owned by the farmers who work it, but Fraser pointed out that there is more land rental north along the Okanagan River.

While this farm has been in the family for years, George Fraser has had a hard time making ends meet with the family business. Originally he didn't plan to farm; he holds a degree in math and physics from the University of British Columbia. He taught for a few years, but in 1965, he decided to go into farming with his dad. "That lasted five years," he explained. "I went deep in the hole and I went back to teaching for seven years. Now I'm a full-time farmer again." He produces apples, cherries, peaches and pears—and like every farmer, he wonders if he will survive when he doesn't earn enough for his crop to cover his production costs. But for George Fraser there is a safety net, which the cost-cutting B.C. Social Credit government is nervous about removing.

Farmers got assistance from the province when the New Democrats held power from 1972 to 1975. At that time, the government put an agricultural policy in place which has helped many to survive. It began with a "land freeze" which prevented the sale of farmland for non-farm uses. This move not only kept land in farming, but it also stabilized land prices; speculators could not bid up with the expectation that land could be rezoned later for industrial development. This land-use policy might be envied in provinces like Ontario, but it was controversial in B.C., even among farmers. Many of them saw their land as an investment toward their retirement and wanted to retain the option of selling. Other farmers had a more immediate concern about the land freeze, feeling that if the land were to remain in agriculture, it was only fair that farmers were able to make a living from it, as an incentive to stay in farming. Faced with that challenge, the NDP government responded with its Farm Income Assurance Plan. Under the plan, farmers, pay premiums and receive payouts when the price of a crop falls below their cost of production. The only exceptions to this are farmers who are paid according to cost-of-production formulas set up by the four national marketing boards.

Many B.C. farmers believe that without this assurance plan, there would be an epidemic of bankruptcy in the fruit business. Political expediency has forced the Social Credit government to keep the farm programme in place, even though Fraser says the province "has been less reasonable" about the levels of financial support the farmer ought to have. However, he doesn't think the programme will disappear. Many farmers are Socred supporters, which puts the provincial government in the embarrassing position of having to back up a popular farm policy put in place by the opposition NDP.

Nevertheless, government legislation has not helped to organise B.C.'s chaotic system of fruit marketing. In fact, the provisions of the Income Assurance Plan may have helped to make that situation worse. Historically, growers in B.C. have tried hard to organise their market, and on paper, they have a plan that's better than any other fruit-growing province. In 1939, farmers successfully lobbied the provincial government for the passage of the B.C. Marketing Act, which set up a Central Selling Desk for fruit. Under this system, all sellers had to ship their product through the new

B.C. Tree Fruit Agency so that every farmer would get the same average price for fruit based on supply and demand. The law governing the agency technically forbids private deals made by growers directly with packers or shippers. But the law is routinely evaded. "Our system worked in 1939 because there was no transport out of the valley, only rail," says Fraser. "With the roads, there are now more big markets for us in cities." It was after the war that the central selling system began to break down; the rapid expansion of transportation and markets during that period made farmers believe they could get a better deal if they found their own customers for fruit.

The postwar years have also brought many immigrants into the B.C. fruit-growing areas. "Few people have roots in this industry," Fraser explained. "And each new wave of immigration has a different idea of marketing." For this reason, many farmers have been technically breaking the law for years by making their own private deals; for example, many growers can get premium prices from some buyers for certain types of apples that produce the colouring most attractive to the consumer. When the NDP government set up the Farm Income Assurance Plan, they helped to weaken the central desk system still further. Their plan allowed people who did not want to use the system to opt out — and to forfeit their right to collect payments under the assurance scheme.

George Fraser is a firm believer in the system because he thinks people can use it to work together for good prices that would help their industry survive. But he's not optimistic. "The system is in the middle of breaking down right now," he says with some resignation. "Those who believe in it are going broke, while others are doing better." In 1983, he earned an average of twenty cents a pound for his fruit. From his total earnings, he has to subtract wages — he hires twenty to thirty people a year to pick apples and cherries — and the costs of irrigation, spraying and pruning. That amounts to fourteen cents out of every twenty, or almost three-quarters of his earnings. Farmers who have ignored the central selling desk are getting as much as fifty cents a pound, or close to six hundred dollars a tonne. "My principles cost me $24,000 dollars that year," he said ruefully. "In order to work, the central selling desk needs a reasonable volume of fruit to sell. But by the time the system is in gear, the local market is filled."

The reason for this is simple: a large chunk of the market is flooded by US imports. Because many farmers worry that their fruit won't be ready in time to meet this competition, "the guy on the truck will come in early and clear out" with some growers' crops before the central selling desk is in full operation. Many local growers expected that the lower Canadian dollar would make it less profitable to bring in the fruit from California and Washington State. "But they are in [with their crop] earlier," Fraser remarked. "And so they control the market. And you don't have to ship a single pound of fruit. All they do is quote a price to Safeway and then, *we* have to match *their* price."

The farm policies put in place by the former NDP government have been a mixed blessing and many growers would be just as happy to do business without financial assistance from government programmes. "I think supply-management has to be a route," Fraser says. But he also points out that the idea of setting quotas and paying farmers according to their costs of production "is not a new idea in the fruit industry." With the present topsy-turvy state of the market, it is hard to imagine that a majority of farmers would agree on such a system. But meanwhile, George Fraser continues to lose money at his farm business. When I asked him if he expected his farm to make it through the financial crunch, he promptly said, "No!" and laughed the way people do who are trying hard to make the best of a bad situation. "If someone offered me the right amount, I would be absolutely stupid not to sell," he said a little more seriously. But it was easy to sense that he really didn't want to quit; his own comments confirmed this. "I'm not sick of farming," he said, smiling a little. "I'm sick of not being paid for it."

The Okanagan Valley is the area best known for fruit production, but the Fraser Valley just east of Vancouver is also a centre of intensive cultivation of both fruit and vegetable crops. Most of these farms belong to commercial growers, who produce a very large volume of fruit on small acreages. About an hour's drive from Vancouver and just before the exit for Abbotsford, there is a huge sign on the south side of the highway which reads: "The Raspberry Capital of Canada." The sign was put up by the Raspberry Growers' Association which represents a group of farmers who are part of a small but genuine success story. At a time when much of the news from the farm is far from optimistic, Canada's western raspberry growers are prospering. This country now exports more processed raspberries than it imports. Ninety percent of the crop is grown within a twenty to thirty-mile stretch of the lower Fraser Valley, just north of the US border. Raspberries may be the only locally-grown fruit crop that can hold its own against the volume of US imports. Raspberry producers in the Fraser raise thirty million pounds of fruit; eleven million pounds of that crop is sold to the processing market in the US. (The states of Washington and Oregon produce twelve millon pounds of berries each). B.C.'s raspberry growers are also starting to export their crop to Japan.

Helmut Sawatsky is one of the farmers who has done well in the raspberry business. I drove up to his house in Abbotsford; it was located on what looked like a quiet residential street, full of split-level bungalows and small fenced-in lawns and gardens. I thought at first I had come to the wrong place. But in fact, this deceptively suburban-looking neighbourhood belongs to small fruit growers whose fields are tucked away behind their houses, out of sight of the street. Sawatsky is a fair-haired man, relaxed and friendly; he's happy about the success of the raspberry business but he's not complacent about the economic problems he shares with other farmers. Sawatsky came to the Fraser from Manitoba; in 1961, his father started the berry operation which he has been managing for the past seven years. He pointed out that most raspberry farmers grow no more than ten to fifteen acres of fruit; some of them work at it part-time, while others have two to five acres of berries as part of a mixed farm.

It's an expensive crop to raise; the delicate fruit has to be hand-harvested. What gives growers the incentive to produce the berries is the unique soil profile of this small corner of the Fraser Valley. Raspberries require sandy soil, but they love a type of gravelly subsoil only found here and in the two states to the south.

People who buy fresh or processed raspberries at the supermarket are often stunned by how much they can cost. Sawatsky explains that even with small acreages, farmers use about six basic pieces of machinery, and even part-time farmers have to make these investments. He adds that most of the farmers in the Fraser Valley are working part-time, with the exception of the few who own several hundred acres of land. Nevertheless, the raspberry business is expanding. In 1981, Fraser Valley growers produced seventeen million pounds of the fruit; in three years, that amount has doubled. There are two large co-ops in the area that wash, clean and freeze about ninety percent of the berries grown in the lower Fraser that are shipped for export. His own co-op takes over half the total berry crop. Because they deal with almost all of the growers, the two co-ops function as a *de facto* central-desk seller which gets all growers the same average price for their berries. Because the co-ops are doing a big-volume business, there is an incentive for them to return good prices to the growers. Even so, there has been some interest in setting up a raspberry growers' marketing board; farmers who support that idea point out that they can't predict the price they will get each year and this makes it difficult to plan for the following season.

The problem raspberry growers are now facing comes from their competitors south of the border. Raspberry growers in the US successfully launched an anti-dumping suit against the Fraser Valley growers; they won their suit by arguing that the B.C. government's Income Assurance Plan is a form of subsidy which gives Canadian farmers an unfair economic advantage. The US Department of Commerce placed a duty on the berries and in June 1985, the US International Trade Commission upheld the growers' claim that their sales had been injured by Canadian imports. While the duty is a relatively small one,[1] it will no doubt make some berry farmers ask just how serious the U.S. really is about bilateral free trade. Like hog farmers whose exports are now subject to duties, berry producers are concerned about the US accusation that Canadian provincial stabilisation plans are illegal trade subsidies.

This annoys Helmut Sawatsky; he is quick to point out that farmers who pay premiums into this Assurance Plan are paid only when the price they get for berries is lower than what it costs them to grow the crop. It is, in fact, insurance, rather than a handout. "We don't rely on the Assurance Plan to keep us in business," Sawatsky explains. We have had some very high prices and we have only made three claims; the plan is not that lucrative. But it *is* essential for hog producers and apple growers—they really depend on it. We are different." He explains that the Socred government has tried to cut back on income assurance, but the B.C. Federation of Agriculture has been strongly opposed to any changes. The Federation is composed of member groups, including the B.C. Raspberry Growers' Association; Sawatsky is president of the latter group which administers the Assurance Plan for the growers and keeps track of market trends in the business.

Even with price fluctuations, these growers have a competitive edge because the type of land they farm is relatively scarce. For this reason, Sawatsky supports the B.C. land freeze, even though he knows that some local farmers who are close to Vancouver's commercial land would rather become rich by selling their farms to developers. "The freeze is here to stay," he says. "Our land base here is so limited. We have the valley—but we're surrounded by the mountains and the sea, and then there is the US border [just a mile away]. We are very confined ... and besides, only three percent of B.C.'s land is arable."

Local farmers get help not only from the land freeze but also from co-operative lending agencies. According to Sawatsky, banks are happy to lend money to raspberry growers and, as far as he knows, they have not called any loans. "Back when I started in 1976," he told me, "I had to explain everything to the bank. Now that the crop has become commercially viable, I can get anything," he added cheerfully.

In fact, the processed raspberry business has grown into a twenty million dollar industry. Its products include a new raspberry juice that Sawatsky thinks could use up the surpluses that sometimes push down the farmer's price in a good crop year. Even with the US duty, the raspberry growers are a genuine Canadian success story, some good news in the risky business of a farming a specialised crop.

The few prosperous B.C. farmers who produce luxury crops get lost in the farm disaster headlines. When prices drop, most farmers in that province can get help from government programmes which assure them a modest living. For an Ontario resident used to hearing about farm-price woes, B.C.'s Income Assurance Programme looks like an intelligent solution to the problem. But no farmer wants to live on handouts. Are most of B.C.'s fruit growers permanently handicapped by accidents of geography and climate from making a good living on the North American market? Is government assistance just an admission that fruit market prices are effectively controlled by the US? Since B.C. fruit often costs more to produce, an early good-sized US crop can push the price down. Is it impossible for B.C.'s fruit growers to fill much of the demand of their local market and earn a good living? To its everlasting credit, B.C.'s former government has decided to save farmland and to help farmers stay afloat. With fierce import competition, it is a glum fact that only programmes like the B.C. plan will keep many of these farmers in business.

Part II: The Problems According to the Farmer

5

Bankers and the Farm Crisis

The twin towers of the Royal Bank of Canada dominate the
southwest corner of Bay and Wellington Streets in Toronto's
downtown financial district. The glass structures are insu-
lated in gold leaf, and their design of interlocking squares
gives the building the look of a giant, glittering honeycomb.
Immediately to the east stands the sombre gray steel and
glass structure of the Toronto-Dominion Bank Tower; the
two huge complexes are connected by a labyrinthine under-
ground city of offices, shops and restaurants. I decided to
visit these banks because they are two of Canada's major
agencies which make loans to farmers. After having spoken
to many financially troubled people, I wanted to hear the
bankers' view on the farm lending controversy. Bankers are
an easy target for farmers. They profited when farm interest
rates soared; they have often lent farmers too much money
when times were good. Some farmers have accused bank
managers of persuading them to make large-scale investments which could never pay for themselves. It struck me
that the cause of the farmer's troubles may go far beyond his

relationship with the bank manager. With dramatic changes in farm technology, both farmers and bankers have long assumed that large-scale investment is the only way to keep agriculture healthy. No one bothered to ask how long both farmers and bankers could afford these investments.

Both George Arnold, Manager of Agricultural Services in Ontario for the Royal Bank and Ed Baskier, Assistant General Manager for Agriculture at the T.D. made the banks' approach to these problems very clear. These bankers feel some responsibility for the rash of family farm bankruptcies across Canada over the past few years but do not conclude that they could have done very much to prevent these failures from occurring. Many farmers borrowed money from the banks in the early 1970's when interest rates were relatively low; from our vantage-point, it is hard to see why both farmers and bankers forgot that interest rates could go up sharply. Bankers explain that the story begins long before the recent boom in farm credit.

Ed Baskier of the T.D. Bank filled me in on the details when I went to see him in his 25th floor office, overlooking the Royal Bank towers and the smokestacks of Toronto's Lake Ontario waterfront. Sitting behind his large desk, he explained that the credit extended to farmers in the early Seventies followed a relatively long period during which banks withdrew their money from agriculture. The banks' unwillingness to lend money to farmers dates back to the Depression, when hundreds of farm bankruptcies forced both the provinces and the federal government to pass laws which would help hard-pressed farmers lighten their debt load with the banks. The federal Farm Creditors' Arrangements Act of 1934 called for court arbitration of farm debt when banks threatened foreclosure. The entry of government into the bankers' territory angered the lending agencies; banks and insurance companies, no longer assured of a good return on their farm investment, pulled out of farm lending entirely.

In 1945, the federal government made an effort to help expand agriculture as part of the retooling of the postwar economy. The Farm Improvement Loans Act provided government guarantees on loans made to farmers as an incentive to lenders to invest money in agriculture. By the late 1950's and early 1960's, most provincial governments had set up programmes to lend money to farmers. Many of these programmes overlapped; to co-ordinate these efforts, the federal government set up the Farm Credit Corporation in 1959. The FCC's mandate was to provide loans for farmers who had to make capital investments in land or buildings.[1] The measures helped farmers, but it took a change in the Bank Act in 1967 to bring the banks back into the business of farm lending. Ed Baskier describes it as a cautious re-entry. "It took a while, though, to get banks into agriculture after the sting of the debt-adjustment acts," he said emphatically. "It took a lot of retirements and deaths before they changed their minds."

Bankers clearly dislike this type of government intervention. Over the past five years, farmers have lobbied Ottawa to revive the Depression-era law that allowed the courts to arbitrate disputes with the banks. In late 1984, the Saskatchewan government introduced legislation to call a halt to farm foreclosures for a period of thirteen months. The provincial Conservatives thought the move was a good way to give many farmers a chance to improve their business finances after a severe drought the previous summer. While bankers were critical of the move, they were not the only mortgage-holders affected, since the legislation covered all lenders, including the Farm Credit Corporation, credit unions and private individuals. For many farmers, the moratorium was a welcome relief; in Saskatchewan, mortgages on farm land amount to half of the province's farm debt of five billion dollars.[2]

Farm spending and farm debt have soared since the Depression; much of this can be traced back to changes in the attitudes of both farmers and farm bankers toward borrowing. According to Baskier, "the old-line bankers who dealt with the honest, hard-working farmer didn't really understand marketing changes, such as supply-management." Banks had to help their local managers deal with new problems and new methods of farm marketing. Both bankers and farmers were using techniques of organising and bookkeeping that were badly outdated. "The majority of farmers didn't have an accounting system to give financial data," says Baskier. And apparently, the only thorough records most farmers kept were for tax purposes. Even as late as 1970, Baskier said, "the overwhelming majority of farmers could not produce a balance sheet." According to Baskier, when farmers came in for loans in the early Seventies, the bank "did not have the evidence of a businessman who could give them an audited statement . . . until three years ago, you couldn't get audited statements [from many farmers]."

Bankers pointed out that without financial records to demonstrate a farmer's ability to run a business, the only way banks could risk sizeable loans in the 1970's was by lending money against the rapidly inflating value of the farmer's land. Bankers argue this point vehemently when they are accused of lending money against the exaggerated value of an asset which could never produce enough income for the farmer to pay back the loan. Still, it is fair to ask if the future value of farmland was a good enough reason for banks to lend money so freely to some farmers; if they did not keep records, perhaps the farmers were simply too much of a risk for the banks to support.

The apparent recent eagerness of bankers to lend money to farmers got its real impetus from events which were set in motion long before the expansion of farm credit. A dramatic change in farm technology has taken place over the past forty years; it has made a big impact not only on the farm economy, but on the way that farmers think about the nature of the work they do. The turning point came after the Second World War, when the manufacturing industry returned to civilian production with an expanded capacity to produce high-powered farm machinery. Encouraged by relatively low energy costs in the 1950's, the size and diversity of new farm equipment acted as a prod to farmers to expand their operations. But the machinery was costly; it worked more efficiently on the large tracts of land which farmers had to buy so that the money they could earn from increased crop production would pay for the costs of the new equipment. For three decades after the Second World War, farmers were told by government and university specialists that expansion was the only way to survive and prosper. It was at this point that banks gradually began to expand their credit to a rapidly developing farm economy.[3]

And farming in Canada did grow, impressively. Between 1951 and 1981, the typical farm expanded in size from 113 to 207 hectares, a jump of 83 percent over a thirty-year period. During this time, the value of Canadian farm machinery and other equipment rose from just under two billion dollars to well over seventeen billion. Initially, these big-dollar investments paid off through a boost in farm production. Between 1971 and 1983, the volume of products from Canada's farms rose 27 percent, compared to just under an eleven percent increase in productivity for other Canadian industries. While the cost and value of capital expenses jumped, the number of people employed on the land began to drop dramatically. In 1950, over twenty percent of Canada's population made their living on the farm. By 1980, that figure had shrunk to four and a half percent.[4] Farming had always been a business; now it had become a major industry which bankers were willing to support. But farming had also been a self-sustaining way of life; now, like any other large-scale enterprise, it had become dependent for its existence on the costs and availability of energy and other inputs produced off the farm.

Because the mechanization of farming has taken place gradually over thirty years, it may be hard to realise that farmers did not always rely on big credit to finance their day-to-day operations. Around the time of the Depression, banks often lent money to a farmer to finance a single project; money could be used to buy equipment or land, but a "loan" could also be a thirty-day note for a one hundred dollar purchase of binder twine. Smaller-scale farm machinery required only a limited amount of fuel; fertilizer was often provided by farm animals and crops were frequently grown from seed which farmers saved from the previous year's crop. Today's big machinery needs large quantities of expensive fuel as a tradeoff for the boost it gives to farm production. Farmers who grow only cash crops do not usually keep livestock; instead, they have to buy petroleum-based fertilizers which have gone up in price with the cost of energy. Likewise, farmers now have to purchase new seed each year; today's high-yielding varieties are hybrids which cannot be saved from the previous year's crop because their seed will not reproduce itself. In exchange for greater efficiency, today's farmer has become saddled with debt not only for the purchase of land and machinery, but also for the costly inputs he needs to run the farm.

In fact, farm debt totals almost 21 billion dollars—a jump of seventeen percent over the past 3 years. The Farm Credit Corporation, the major federal lending agency for farmers, recently released a survey which showed that a typical farmer runs an operation worth $508,000, against which he owes an average of $91,000. But the value of that farmer's operation may be inflated; the real net worth of farmers in Canada has fallen by a total of $4.2 billion since 1981. According to the FCC survey, for each year between 1981 and 1984, the net income of farmers was even lower than the annual drop in the farmer's net worth. In other words, while the farmer's income continues to drop, the value of his share in the investment in its business has dropped also.[5] And that lower equity limits the amount of money a farmer can borrow against the worth of his operation. Because farm incomes are so insecure from year to year, a farmer cannot use his earnings as security to guarantee his loans.

This was not the way farming looked in the 1970's, when a more prosperous economy allowed farmers to turn for help to the banks. It was a period of great expansion in farm borrowing; a strong economy and confidence in agribusiness were pushing up the price of land and farmers were not afraid to purchase an asset that promised to increase in value over the years.With land values rising, a farmer's share in the equity (or financial investment) in his land would increase as well. It was because of this that the farmer was able to borrow funds for farm machinery against the rising value of his land. And the farmer's bank manager believed that his bank, in turn, had a secure investment. Interest rates at the time were relatively low—under ten percent. By comparison, the average prices paid to farmers for their products were rising at a rate of over fifteen percent a year. Land values were going up faster than the interest rate; capital gains earned by anyone who owned land were rising even faster than the income of the farmer. This climate for expansion was a mixed blessing; farms grew larger, but speculators also put money into land and pushed prices up still further.[6] Young people who wanted to farm found it difficult to afford land; they went into considerable debt because they believed that their future in business could be secured by owning land that was sure to increase in value.

Today, most farm borrowing is done for mortgages on buildings and land. About 20 percent of all bank loans to farmers are short-term, to be paid within eighteen months. These loans cover operating expenses, including seed, chemicals and fertilizer. Intermediate-term loans for periods up to ten years make up about 30 percent of farm lending. These loans are for the purchase of larger items such as machinery and livestock, or for farm building improvement. Long-term loans involve mortgages for land and buildings; slightly over half of all bank loans to farmers are in this category.[7] Still, that figure represents only about 27 percent of all long-term credit; close to 40 percent of these loans come from the FCC, while farmers also borrow smaller amounts from provincial government programmes, credit unions and various private sources.[8] But farmers get most of their short and intermediate-term credit from the chartered banks.[9] Each bank varies in the amount of money it will invest in farm loans; while two to three percent of all loans at the T.D. Bank go to farmers, the Royal Bank estimates that it invests about fifteen percent of all loans in agriculture. Some farmers borrow at the slightly lower prime interest rate usually reserved by the banks for their most reliable business or professional customers. Most borrow at interest rates which are one or two percent above the prime rate. Nevertheless, all farmers were hurt by the sudden interest rate jump in the early Eighties, especially those who had to renew the terms of their mortgages at the higher rates. Banks were unconcerned about the possibility of a jump in interest rates during the credit boom of the Seventies because they assumed that the farmer's land assets would also increase in time. For this reason, banks lent some farmers as much as five hundred thousand dollars. In 1971, Canadian farmers borrowed one billion dollars; by 1984, that debt figure had grown to eight billion. The value of farm land and buildings has not kept pace with the level of debt, as the banks had hoped they would.

This problem became acute in 1981, when interest rates soared to twenty percent.[10] Bankers speak about this spiral with a detachment we usually reserve for natural catastrophes. George Arnold, the Royal's Manager for Ontario Agricultural Services tried to explain what happened to push interest rates up. I met him in his office, which was separated by a glass wall from a large open area filled with office workers and banks of computer terminals. He's a friendly man, the image of a solid banker in his gray three-piece suit. He views soaring interest rates in part as the result of the flow of Canadian capital into profitable US investment; he also links those higher rates with the "fight against inflation" launched by the US government. He agreed that high rates of government spending in both countries had pushed interest rates up and it is a fact that the US deficit has doubled since President Reagan took office.[11] The point is not lost on farmers. One disgruntled tobacco grower told me that "our farm equity is being transferred into the US defence budget." Trying to pinpoint the cause of high interest rates, the farmer added, "One bank put about twenty million dollars in one day into the US money market. Where do you draw the line on decency?"[12]

Farmers ask that question because when the drain on the money supply pushed up the costs of borrowing, they were the ones who were caught in the squeeze. Red meat producers faced with low prices suffered most from the interest rate jump. Farmers and bankers both understand the reasons behind the rise in interest rates, although their approaches to the problem have little in common. Bankers are engaged in a kind of balancing act involving relatively abstract ideas about economics and the money supply, while farmers cannot distance themselves from the every day effects. Bankers themselves may have been able to do little about climbing interest rates, but they were nevertheless able to benefit from them; banks made record profits when higher borrowing rates added to the depression in the farm economy.[13] Bankers like George Arnold are well aware that farmers are having a hard time. He suggested that there could be intervention to stop another interest rate spiral. "I doubt it would happen again," he remarked. "A lot of people are just hanging on and government would not allow it to happen."

However, the federal government has not taken action to curb interest rates on farm loans, in spite of a vocal farm lobby. Ottawa sees farm problems as relatively minor compared to more widespread urban unemployment and small business failures. Finance Minister Michael Wilson's 1985 budget offered farmers little more than a major incentive to quit the business. The new capital gains exemptions give farmers preferential treatment; they may sell their farms immediately without having to pay tax on the profits. Farm groups urged Ottawa to help them get new sources of low-interest funding, but the request was ignored in the budget. Farmers had hoped for the introduction of agribonds to attract investment both from retiring farmers and from the commercial money market. Provincial agriculture ministers across the country supported the idea of the bonds; their low interest rate would give a good return as a tax-exempt investment. Many provincial politicians also liked the agribond idea because they felt it would amalgamate the maze of government farm-assistance programmes into a single package.[14] But Ottawa clearly felt that the farmer did not need this sort of assistance.

Bankers may also hold that view. In 1981, the Canadian Bankers' Association stated that only 0.5 percent of all Canadian farmers were in trouble. By 1984, the Farm Credit Corporation determined that this figure had risen to seventeen percent.[15] At any rate, farmers' difficulties are viewed differently by each bank; while nine to ten percent of the Royal's farm loans are in arrears, payments may be as little as a month behind—not in the Bank's view an indication that these farms are going to fail. At the T.D. Bank, just over four percent of all farm borrowers had one or more loans that

were ninety days overdue by the end of 1984. Ed Baskier
points out that close to half of the T.D.'s farm customers
didn't borrow at all that year; according to him, many of
them deposited money and he insists "there's money out
there." Loans at the FCC tell another story; 12 percent of all
borrowers from the federal agency had loans in arrears at
the end of 1984. Many of the FCC's 79,000 customers are high
risk cases. Unlike the chartered banks, the FCC's mandate
requires it to give loans to farmers who cannot obtain funding
from other sources.[16] About half the funds lent by the FCC
for long-term credit are now outstanding in loans worth
about four billion dollars.

Whereas farm bankruptcies are declared by the business
itself, a foreclosure is initiated by the bank against a customer
who is seriously behind in payments of loans. George Arnold
explained that before the Royal forecloses on a farm, it
has to be up to a year behind on its loan or mortgage
payments. His bank also forecloses in serious cases when
they have "lost confidence in the ability of the farmer to
manage his farm. We don't come out on top," he adds. "We
have had some horrendous losses." Both the T.D. and the
Royal insist that they have not accumulated much of a land
inventory because of farm foreclosures. However, the FCC
foreclosed on 394 farms during the 1983-84 fiscal year. Because
of these high numbers, Federal Agriculture Minister John
Wise called for an evaluation of the FCC's practices; the
agency placed a brief moratorium on foreclosures from
November 1984 to early January 1985. When the moratorium
was lifted, a small change was made to benefit farmers.
The FCC's provincial boards which hear appeals from farmers
who are turned down for loans may now hear appeals of
foreclosures if the farmer requests it.[17]

Farm bankruptcy and foreclosure figures look alarming.
Yet bankers don't believe the situation is as grave as farmers
describe it. George Arnold estimates that small business
foreclosures at the Royal Bank are about four times higher
than what farmers have faced. But he also points out that
traditionally, small business always has a much higher failure
rate than agriculture. "Five or six of every ten that start up
fail," he adds. He explains that in the past, farm failure rates

were low because the capital investments made to start up the business were small. This made farming a relatively secure way of life and a small business which, unlike others, had some protection against bankruptcy. "Agriculture has had more stability," says Arnold. "Business is used to being highly capitalised. Now agriculture is more highly capitalised and so now there's more failure." Ed Baskier at the T.D. is irked by the publicity farm foreclosures have received over the past few years. Reacting with annoyance to a New York *Times* story about farm troubles in the US, he described its dire warnings as "a cancer that just won't go away." He feels strongly that the media has distorted reports of farm hardships and that the number of farm bankruptcies and foreclosures is not as significant as it appears. "We don't consider these [failures] an epidemic," he says. "Nature is saying, 'agriculture—you must restructure and make some changes.'" He believes that the banks could not have forseen the problems in today's farm economy, pointing out that farmers had it relatively good only a few years back.

Faced with a tight economy, farmers still have to pay their loans and other bills, while farm lenders have to answer to their shareholders and bank directors. Farmers borrow money to support what they see as a fundamental business—one which includes a way of life, woven into the social fabric of a rural community. The farm lender wants to know if investment in agriculture will mean profits for the bank. Ed Baskier made it clear that bankers view farming exactly as they would view any other enterprise with money-making potential. "In any business," he points out, "investors look at the appreciation and the dividends." He takes a dollars-and-cents view of a farmer's success, commenting that the increasing value of farm assets has been "substantial." A recent survey shows that even with a drop in real farm income from ten years ago, the value of land, buildings and equipment for the average farmer is four times greater now.[18] And while the province of Ontario had the second-highest bankruptcy rate in Canada in 1984 (it lost 154 farms), a provincial survey suggests that most full-time farmers there are getting by—or, at least, not going broke.

Herb Driver, an agricultural economist at the University of Guelph, conducts the annual Ontario Farm Management Analysis Project; his most recent survey was based on data gathered from farm financial records filed in 1983. He counted in only full-time farmers—according to Revenue Canada's definition which states that, for tax purposes, a "farmer" must earn a minimum annual income of $2,500 a year from the sale of his products.[19] Many part-time farmers not included in the survey are those in financial trouble who have been forced to supplement their farm income; their absence explains why this survey is relatively optimistic. It points out that one in twenty of Ontario's full-time farmers are in trouble for expanding too quickly in the 1970's; many of these are beef feedlot operators. The average net income of an Ontario beef producer is just over $31,000, and the top third with the highest earnings have an average net income of $56,074.[20] If these top-earning beef producers are averaged into the total, earnings at the lower and of the scale may be poor. Ontario's pork producers who raise weaners— piglets bred and sold to be fattened up for market—lost an average of close to six thousand dollars each in 1983. Pork producers who raised their piglets up to market weight and then sold them earned a net income of $16,604—not the picture of a thriving farm commodity group, by any standards.

The survey also reveals that Ontario's most prosperous farmers operate mixed farms made up of livestock and cash crops. Their average net income was close to $30,000; their top third earners clear $69,489 a year[21]—a fact worth noticing at a time when many farms have become highly specialised with costly capital investment. According to the T.D. Bank, most Canadian farmers do produce more than one commodity. And while that may not be a very "mixed" farm in the traditional sense, bankers still feel better about lending money to a farm with at least two commodities. Ed Baskier points out that "as a lender, you try to assess the risk, and you are more comfortable with a feeder hog operation with a feed-producing base"—in other words, a farm which can raise its own grain to feed hogs, allowing the farmer to cut back on his operating costs.

The farm financial picture is not rosy, but 1984 turned out to a relatively good year for farm income. Canada's farmers earned twenty billion dollars in gross income that year — a figure just slightly larger than what it cost farmers to operate their businesses in 1984. Ironically, the prairie drought gave a boost to the income figure; because the crop was poor, farmers got good prices for feed grain, and sold much of their stored grain from other years. Prairie farmers also received well over two hundred million dollars in federal stabilisation payments to compensate them for crop losses. In the Maritimes and Ontario, good weather helped farm crops and pushed up profits, but for 1985, it is estimated that seven out of ten provinces will see a drop in farm income — a sobering fact when we consider that even with 1984's higher income, farm bankruptcies rose.[22] It is not hard to understand why some farmers felt discouraged that year if their only chance to make a profit came when crop failures triggered payments under a government insurance programme.

No one questions that Canadian farmers are up against some serious economic difficulties. Some farm groups blame the banks for making so much credit available to the farmer in the 1970's, without being prudent enough to realise that interest rates might change abruptly. But why did some banks lend huge amounts of money to farmers who seldom kept financial records in the first place? How did these bankers judge farmers' business skills? George Arnold of the Royal Bank: "Our purpose was one of analysing expansion and we share some responsibility for the credit situation," he says. "But I'm not prepared to accept the fact that bankers did any arm-twisting." He admits that high interest rates "certainly helped bank profits. But they were accruing from other places than agriculture." Ed Baskier acknowledges some responsibility for the runaway lending policies of the 1970's; he says that "unsound business decisions were made by bankers and lenders" at that time. He mentioned that net income on the farm started dropping in 1976 and that "we should have put the brakes on. No one saw the bubble about to burst." But he believes that even if his bank had reduced its farm lending, it would not have affected the easy credit situation. "We were working in a competitive environment," he says. "We preached financial management—but no one would come to church."

However the banks view the matter, farmers are left living with the mistakes of the 1970's credit boom. Many farmers have lost equity in their operations because land values are starting to drop, while the interest on their debts for the land still remains high. When I raised this issue with Ed Baskier, he reacted strongly, saying he knew banks have been accused of lending too much money against inflated land values. "The value of land is now being pushed down by farmers who are reluctant to buy it," he added. But in some cases, land values dropped rapidly; in Ontario's Bruce and Grey counties, where many farmers have been foreclosed, excess land suddenly on the market pulled down land values for everyone. I have never received a direct answer from anyone when I've asked if it was fair that farmers who were not being foreclosed should see their land devalued because their neighbours had gotten in trouble with the bank. But among the many problems faced by farmers, one of the largest is the fact that no politicians or lending institutions are willing to come to terms with the effects of an uncertain economy.

In looking to the future, Ed Baskier agrees with farmers when he says "there is hardly a thing wrong with agriculture that income wouldn't fix." That, at least, would be a start. "But for most people," he added, "the cost of food equals the cost of living and that is pure, unadulterated garbage." While I had to agree that Canadian consumers do not pay what it really costs to produce their food, it was not clear to me how these bankers would approach the problem of getting more income from the marketplace. Baskier, for one, disagrees vehemently with the idea of supply-management. "There are a lot of smug people hiding" behind that system, he said, adding that for milk, egg and poultry farmers, "the most significant part of their capital investment is in their quota." While the quota system allows these farmers to earn back their costs of production, Baskier doesn't think this fact justifies the high capital expense, especially when it might hold back young people who want to get into the business. "The high cost of quota is the capital sin of supply-management against the young farmer," Baskier said. Canada's bankers have gone on record as stating that higher income is the one best solution for what ails the farm economy. If that won't work, Ed Baskier has another solution. "Farm land prices have to come down to meet a realistic level of income," he says. "Food prices are being set on a world market and the marketplace is reducing the price of land. Land has to pay for itself, but income can't cover its cost." But since Canadian farmers must sell their products on the world market, how will they solve their low-income problem? Wayne Easter, dairy farmer and president of the eight-thousand member National Farmers' Union says his organization supports quotas and supply-management for all farmers. "More farmers are in favour of it now than they were five or ten years ago," he says. "We are gradually moving in that direction."[23]

Whatever the outcome for farming, bankers have many perceptions about its future that go against some deeply-felt ideas farmers hold about what they need to do a good job as farmers. One of these assumptions involves the place of land both as a productive investment and as an important part of the farmer's role as a cultivator of the soil and the director of his own business. George Arnold of the Royal Bank suggests that young farmers might try going into the business without owning any land. "If I were just starting out in agriculture, I would rent my land requirements," he said, "and I would use capital to buy assets that would produce a bigger return. It's best to establish your equity and net worth [before buying land]." The idea makes sense; both bankers and farmers recognise how difficult it is for young people to get into farming with today's relatively high land costs. George Arnold admitted that when land is owned by speculators and rented out to farmers, it "maybe doesn't get the same care and attention it would get if it were theirs the rest of their lives." Even land rental won't make for more efficient farming if other farm costs are high. "Many of the hardest hit are the larger farms, because machinery costs are out of line," says George Arnold, while Ed Baskier points out that often, very large farm operations are not as economical as a more moderate-sized family farm business.

Whether they own or rent land, many farmers are forced to earn some of their income off the farm. And while bankers see part-time farming as a necessary trend, farmers often do it reluctantly, feeling angry that they should have to accommodate themselves to a poor farm income by taking a second job. The practice of overworking rented soil with the same cash-crop year after year to make ends meet also depletes a non-renewable resource—the topsoil. When I raised these concerns with Ed Baskier, I realized immediately that he understood what I meant. The serious and rather stern expression on his face changed; he looked reflective, and for the first time in our conversation he started to speak more freely. "We sometimes find ourselves in a role playing God," he said. "It's more than we want to carry. We don't always know where our responsibility stops and starts." He leaned forward as he spoke. "I would hate to be guilty of lending money to an erosion situation, to bad husbandry. There are social issues here, and we want to be conscious of them. It's very difficult." He sat back in his chair and cupped his chin in his hand. "The bank has walked away with a reasonably clear conscience," he said thoughtfully. "Some people did get hurt by some poor lending policy. But we can look our shareholders in the eye and say we think we were being responsible." He spoke carefully, as though he were still turning the issue over in his mind. And then he summed it up. "The truth is," he said, "that in the marketplace, if we allow people to succeed, then we also allow them to fail."

6
The World Market: Imports and Exports

Apart from the policies of banks, the urban shopper is the easiest target for farmers who feel frustrated about their inability to make a good living. Most farmers correctly identify a federal government "cheap food policy" as a major problem, and we see the results of that policy at the supermarket, in the form of cheap imports, processing and packaging costs and retail pricing policies. Here, many farmers feel helpless to make any substantive changes. Few farmers have the opportunity to take a systematic look at the connections between import policies, retail pricing, the role of corporate agribusiness, food speculation and government policy, and how they combine to erode the economic position of the farmer. Instead, farmers have often been encouraged by government, bankers and some farm organisations to lay all the blame on the greedy consumer, whose sole interest lies in obtaining the cheapest food possible.

Over the past few years, Agriculture Canada has developed policies for what it calls the "agri-food sector," of which agriculture is only a single part. In a recent policy paper,[1] this sector is described as including "input suppliers, farmers, processors, distributors and retailers, and governments." Ottawa thus ties the future of Canadian food marketing to the export trade and the report tells us that it is possible for Canada to "nearly double the output of the agri-food sector" with the proper strategy. The report shows that Agriculture Canada puts as much emphasis on the development of non-farm food businesses as it does on the farming.[2] Agriculture already plays a large role in Canada's export trade. Grain is Canada's largest export, giving Canada a food-trade surplus of $4 billion. Because we are such a productive grain-growing country, Agriculture Canada is enthusiastic about grain exports; the Canadian Wheat Board, the federal agency which handles wheat sales has encouraged farmers to grow more than their mid-1970s average of fifteen million tonnes a year.

The Board also said Canada's farmers could produce thirty million tonnes of wheat by 1985. Farmers went along with the plan, and reached that goal a year early, with intensive farming and the working of marginal land which otherwise might not have been put into the production of grain.[3] Because of this export potential, Canadian agriculture looks quite good on paper. But ironically, while Canada produces huge volumes of grain for the world market, we import many other crops which our farmers once raised themselves, because they just can't afford to grow them now. While locally-grown produce may taste better, it cannot always compete with the low-cost production of the same crop in other countries. A Canadian farmer who grows strawberries or peaches has to slash his prices to compete with cheaper imports from the US where energy costs are cheaper; he also competes with Third World countries which often pay low wages for farm help. It may come as a surprise to learn that at the end of the Second World War, Canada was self-sufficient in the production of plums, peaches, apricots, strawberries and pears. By 1980, we were importing over half of our peaches and close to three-quarters of our plums, as well as close to half our supply of the other three fruits.[4]

How have we come to import crops we can produce ourselves? In most cases, today's farmer has to produce the limited number of crops that are "competitive" on the world market—unless, of course, he runs a very small local operation. Ottawa's farm export policy clearly has its benefits in terms of trade, but it also sets a certain agenda for the direction agriculture is taking. This involves the corporate view of the food system, where food is produced only where it is profitable and not necessarily where it is needed most. From all accounts Agriculture Canada accepts this line of thinking, and so does the US Department of Agriculture which helped initiate the global food import-export pattern we have today. On the face of it, that pattern looks bizarre; while many of us know that the industrialized countries (including the EEC) export huge food surpluses, most of us don't realize that just about every underdeveloped country (except Mexico and Venezuela) is a net exporter of food.[5]

These Third World exporters include African countries in the drought-stricken lands south of the Sahara; nine out of the twenty-two countries asking the UN Food and Agriculture Organization for emergency food aid in October 1983 were all net exporters of food.[6] While this sounds strange, it is also true that export trade is to some degree a form of barter; Third World countries sell their produce in order to gain the foreign exchange abroad which will help them buy Western goods and technology. Our own locally-grown food meets stiff competition from many of these imports. And farmers who sell to processors at home must think about the world market price for crops. It is a situation that leaves many farmers feeling they have little control over their incomes or the future of their businesses.

The fact that big-volume food imports routinely cross borders also points to an unprecedented change in diet around the world to a uniform North American style of eating. While no one planned at first to make such a major change in the world's eating habits, it became the logical result of policies followed by the US Department of Agriculture in the late 1940s. At the end of the Second World War, the US developed a grain surplus at a time when the agriculture of many other countries was in ruins. With the changeover from horsepower to mechanised farming now complete, farmers no longer felt restricted in the amount of land they could cultivate.[7] Cheap fuel added to the productivity of this new style of farming. Nitrogen surpluses from munitions factories went into the production of chemical fertilizers;[8] these included the commonly used anhydrous ammonia, a chemical used in wartime to compact the soil for air-landing strips in the jungles.[9] This technology, combined with new seed hybrids gave the US farmer huge bumper crops of corn and other grains which they started to feed to livestock in an effort to get rid of the surplus. North Americans soon became fond of steak and roast beef dinners, as the supply of cheap red meat rose. The USDA believed that the only way to unload this vast agricultural surplus was to promote a North American style of eating abroad. US food aid policy was set up "to promote the foreign policy of the US, to combat hunger and dispose of surpluses."[10] And the USDA went further; they set up promotional campaigns throughout Asia to push bread and other baked goods in countries which grew little or no wheat. Today, the Third World accounts for over one-half the world's wheat market. The postwar history of US food policy has already been well documented in Dan Morgan's landmark study of the grain trade, *Merchants of Grain;* it includes a disturbing look at how the US Department of Agriculture almost singlehandedly altered the dietary habits of Iran in the 1960s.

Even these policies, however, didn't get rid of all the US farm surpluses. Other industrialized countries were accumulating surpluses of their own as their agriculture also became more mechanised. The US still had cheap grain surpluses that Europeans no longer needed, and their only potential market was the Third World. Because many less-developed countries had no foreign exchange to purchase the crops, the US decided to accommodate new customers by taking payment for grain in their almost-worthless local currency. The US then returned the funds to its customers, extracting a promise that the buyer would use the cash for industrial development. The result was a ready market for cheap grain. Large numbers of people, lured by jobs in the cities, gave up farming with the approval of their governments and their "tied" purchase of US grain. Eventually, the surpluses started to run out, and with the massive US sale of grain to the Soviet Union in 1973, world grain prices jumped. The new urban poor of Third World countries, led to believe that bread was a sign of wealth, had lost their staple crops and were now going hungry. Cheap imports had made many countries neglect agricultural development,[11] locking them into a cycle of poverty and hunger.

Huge grain imports have often been accompanied by large exports of nutritious local crops, once consumed as part of the native diet. India, for example, was a net exporter of fruit, tea, spices, sugar and coffee each year between 1976 and 1981, and Japan is heavily dependent on expensive Western food imports, while it exports its own surplus of rice, the grain staple of the traditional Asian diet. Fresh fish which once provided protein for Africans is now exported to Europe; canned fish from Morocco and Ghana now ends up in North American cat food.[12] One expert points out that farming in many Third World countries is dominated by corporate agribusiness which pays low wages; in such countries, labour-intensive field crops are grown in large quantities for export. On the other hand, North America's grain production for export is capital-intensive, because it uses large-scale technology for its huge croplands.[13] In short, agriculture now operates much like any other worldwide industry. While food has always been a necessity for life and a reflection of cultural differences, it has now become another commodity, to be produced only in those areas where costs are low enough to make a profit. To my knowledge, the unsettling effects of such a policy have not been studied by any agriculture ministry, even though the loss of agriculture has created a starvation in the Third World and economic hardship in our own country.

Many farmers already know that when they specialize for the export market, they can end up damaging their soil through continuous monocropping without the rotations of less profitable crops that could build up their soil once again. In Saskatchewan, for example, agriculture was once more diversified; now farmers mainly grow wheat, often on marginal land which faces severe erosion.[14] The boom in grain trade has helped Canada push into markets once dominated by the United States, including both China, and the Soviet Union (which is straining its farming capability by trying to adopt the US-style diet of grain-fed meat)[15]. Although we do well with our grain exports, the production of some locally-grown crops has all but disappeared. Between 1930 and 1975, tomato production in British Columbia dropped from close to sixty million pounds to just under ten million pounds.[16] Between 1965 and 1975, canned tomato imports tripled. Meanwhile, Canada's canned peach industry, once a thriving group of small businesses in the Niagara Peninsula, has been wiped out by Australian competition.[17]

Canada now imports well over three billion dollars worth of US food products alone each year, mostly fruit and vegetables. In fact, all imports are on the rise, and a Science Council of Canada study done in 1979 warns us that by the year 2000, Canada could become dependent on other countries for all our food, with the exception of grain, milk, eggs and oilseeds.[18]

It is easy to ignore these setbacks because of the trade surplus earned by Canada's agricultural exports, and the relatively cheap food which many imports provide for the consumer. Yet in 1983, the year Canada's food-trade surplus hit four billion dollars, farm income dropped by $150 million and farm debt jumped to $21 billion.[19] The boost in Canada's export trade hides the fact that to keep competitive on the world market, the farmer must pay a huge price in operating costs for farm fuel, fertilizers and pesticides, plus the interest on the money he borrows to purchase them. Also, because of the stiff import competition all over the world, governments often try to protect farmers with tariffs and other agreements negotiated within the General Agreement on Tariffs and Trade (GATT). But Canada's tariff structure has not done much for Canada's fruit and vegetable growers. In fact, it has been compared to the tariff setup in an underdeveloped country.[20]

Trade rivals such as the US and the EEC countries levy tariffs on produce that are fifty to a hundred percent higher than ours; these are kept in place throughout the year. Canadian tariffs are maintained only while our fresh produce is on the market.[21] While this allows Canadians to eat relatively inexpensive fresh fruits and vegetables all year round, it also hurts our local producers. Canada's short-period tariff on imported peaches, strawberries and grapes allows the US products to arrive on our markets in large quantities before our locally-grown fruit is ready to be picked, thus driving the price down. Imported grapes face a higher tariff in Canada than they do in the US, but our levy is in place for only fifteen weeks,[22] compared to a US period of seven and a half months for grapes. Other US imports, including spinach and melons have no tariff restrictions placed on them by Canada.[23] It is ironic that non-food products are often better protected; importers pay a 6.8 percent tariff to bring in US-made guns and rifles, while an importer of US-made hockey sticks gets hit with a whopping 22.5 percent tariff.[24]

Many Canadian farmers are concerned about US proposals for a free trade agreement with Canada. The plan would eliminate protective tariffs and quotas wherever possible. Canada exports two billion dollars' worth of food to the US, most of it livestock, meat and cereal products,[25] and there is plenty of evidence to suggest that political pressure in the US would work to make free trade with Canada a liability for our country. A recent series of decisions made by the US Department of Commerce has placed duties on hogs and raspberries imported from Canada. These decisions were based on the belief that Canadian stabilisation programmes were, in fact, unfair trade subsidies. Canada's exports of hogs to the US have been growing; in 1984, Canada shipped 25 percent of its total hog production to the US—a total of over one million live hogs and over three hundred million pounds of pork, worth well over five hundred million dollars.[26] But it is worth mentioning that Canada's hog production is no match for the US; even with our large exports, our hogs account for only two and a half percent of their total.[27] Many Canadian hog imports were encouraged by US packers; demand for hogs was high in the US and the lower Canadian dollar made the imports a bargain for them.

In December 1984, the US Department of Commerce imposed a preliminary tariff on Canadian hogs; nevertheless, live hog exports to the US climbed by over fifty percent in the first half of 1985. However, the tariffs now cost Canadian farmers about $10.50 a hog or about ten percent of the selling price. Eventually, hog farmers will simply have to cut back on production to account for the added costs of the duty; some will have to leave the business.[28]

There are far-reaching implications to this tariff. The US Department of Commerce made its ruling against the imports of Canadian pork because it insisted that Canada's system of farm stabilisation payments is in fact an illegal subsidy which protects the farmer from the normal risks of the free market. What they do not mention is the extensive US system of agricultural price supports.[29] While the US plan works differently from ours, it involves government intervention to help the farmer by effectively boosting very low commodity prices. They obviously hoped that Canadians would not notice the deception. But if the US continues to insist that the Canadian programmes are illegal, then Canada might eventually be forced to make radical changes in its stabilisation system. Ironically, the US recently set up an "Agricultural Enhancement Programme"—a fund of two billion dollars set up specifically to subsidise US exports so that their prices will remain competitive against subsidised farm goods sold by the EEC.[30]

Some Canadian hog farmers argue that we should not export our own surplus problem to the US; these pork producers believe that supply-management would prevent hog farmers in either country from flooding the market and pushing down prices for both Canada and the US. And while there are no immediate prospects for a quota system in the red meat business, we do have a number of examples from the past to show us what agricultural "free trade" might mean for Canada. In 1976 and 1977, US hogs flooded the Canadian market, accounting for fourteen percent of the total. As a result, prices for hogs dropped by ten percent. Charles Mayer, the federal Wheat Board Minister, adds that Canada has had little success limiting the flow of US red meat. In 1973, eighty percent of all the cattle slaughtered in Toronto was from the US. Canada tried to limit these imports by placing a temporary surtax on them; as a result, the US simply closed its borders to all Canadian beef.[31]

In December 1984, the Canadian government tried once again to limit imports of beef. But Ottawa backed down and raised its quota limits, this time because the EEC nations threatened to retaliate. In Canada, beef producers maintain that the larger volumes of imports will force them to cut back on their herds to survive, resulting in a shortage of beef during the next decade. Eventually, we will notice the difference when the prices in the supermarket go up.[32]

Imports are not the only problem. Canada's tobacco farmers have been badly treated by the multinational corporations which run their industry. Had their crop been wheat, apples or hogs, there may have been more of a public outcry over what happened to tobacco growers in 1984. Ontario has over two thousand tobacco farmers, most located in the southwestern part of the province. The growers who work these sandy soils produce over ninety percent of the tobacco grown in this country. It is a valuable crop, second only to corn in the revenue it earns for the Ontario farmer.[33] Ontario's 1984 crop was worth $298 million.[34] The vast majority of this tobacco is the "flue-cured" variety used in cigarettes. Much of it is exported; the United Kingdom and the US are the two biggest markets, with the US buying over twenty-five million dollars worth of leaves in 1983. The cigarette industry in Canada is dominated by Imperial Tobacco, which has more than half the share of the Canadian cigarette market. Imperial is, in turn, owned by the multinational Imasco Corporation. In 1983, Imasco earned 45 percent of its two and a half billion dollar revenue from tobacco sales;[35] at the end of March 1984, they had profits of $200 million, an increase of more than $22 million from the previous year.[36]

In 1984, when the Flue-Cured Tobacco Growers' Marketing Board negotiated with Imperial to sell their crop, they were told that the company planned to cut their tobacco purchases by twenty percent. Imperial explained that people were smoking less; they said that tobacco consumption had dropped five percent over the past year. In 1983, the company had bought 215 million pounds of tobacco from the growers; in 1984, they wanted only 170 million pounds.[37] The growers were angry; they blamed both federal and provincial taxes for the drop in cigarette sales, pointing out that both governments collected well over two billion dollars in tobacco taxes in 1983 as they continued to preach about consumer health. They also mentioned that the federal tax on a pack of cigarettes jumped 45 percent over the past four years, while provincial cigarette taxes were up 163 percent over the same period of time.[38]

In 1984, farmers lobbied intensively to get the taxes cut back, warning that if people smoked less, many of the 8,000 spinoff jobs in the planting and harvesting of tobacco could be eliminated.[39] But some astute growers looked at the problem carefully, realising that the drop in smoking could not account for the giant drop in demand for tobacco from cigarette manufacturers. These farmers have come to feel that they are pawns in a tobacco price war being waged on the world market by multinational corporations. Hugh Zimmer grows tobacco in Otterville, just south of Woodstock in southwestern Ontario. Zimmer is an intense person whose living-room floor is covered with file folders and newspaper clippings about the tobacco industry. He is new to farming, having bought his 134-acre farm in 1982, twelve years after he graduated in agriculture from the University of Guelph. He worked for a brokerage firm where he learned more about the economics of agriculture and the business of farming around the world. Profits are his main concern as a business-man; he studied livestock production at Guelph, but he stayed away from it, knowing it was not a money-maker.

Having made a profit at tobacco-growing, he speaks with anger about how the cigarette manufacturers have treated the farmers. Zimmer explains that Imperial Tobacco's parent company, Imasco, is 40 percent controlled by British-American Tobacco, and Britain is now buying much of its tobacco at lower prices from Zimbabwe, putting Ontario farm businesses in jeopardy. He told me that if the Ontario tobacco industry was going to survive, "it would survive in a scaled-down form, which is what the multinationals wish . . . we're in an international tobacco trade war, that's essentially where we are. And we're not alone," he continued, "There's an international grains war going on as well. I feel that people will realize that we are being used as a pawn to attempt to lower the US price for tobacco coming up in the 1985 year by trying to destroy our market system. Then," he added, "the US will have to drop their prices for world tobacco, which will then force Brazil to drop their prices and then Rhodesia [Zimbabwe] will have to drop theirs and it's just a domino effect." When I asked him who the winner was in a tobacco war, he answered without hesitation, "the multinationals. There's no question about that. Their profits haven't even slipped. That's the obscene part of the situation."[40]

Zimmer also says that Imasco puts the largest percentage of its tobacco earnings in Canada into other areas, including the recent purchase of a major US drugstore chain. But he is just as angry at politicians who impose heavy taxes which can put farmers out of business by making cigarettes too costly. That point may seem frivolous to those of us who are concerned about the health effects of smoking. In fact, many Canadians may have been pleased by the recent measures in the federal budget which placed an excise tax of twenty-five cents on a small package of cigarettes. Each province has its own sales tax, so the price of cigarettes will vary across the country. Evidence points to the fact that higher taxes do make people cut back or quit smoking. However, Zimmer points out that tobacco is still a legal product, even though there are some restrictions on its advertising and sale. "If you want us out, give us compensation," he says. Surprisingly, other tobacco growers agree, feeling that governments should get more honest and ban the sale of tobacco instead of promoting health while collecting tax windfalls that could put tobacco farmers out of business. Zimmer insists he has no personal interest in producing tobacco; unlike many farmers, he refuses to grow anything that will not give him back his costs of production. And as far as tobacco is concerned, "I could care less," says Zimmer. "It's just a crop."

Opponents of the tobacco industry have actually spoken up on behalf of tobacco farmers and their right to earn a living producing alternative crops. Dr. Alex McPherson, President of the Canadian Medical Association, points out that governments ought to give up their big tax profits from tobacco products and instead, move toward a programme to help tobacco farmers switch crops.[41] It has also been suggested that a special tax could be levied on cigarettes as a government subsidy to farmers to get them out of the tobacco business.[42] And tobacco farmers already know that the sandy soils where tobacco grows best are ideal for many other cash crops—including tomatoes, cucumbers, strawberries and even new varieties of peanuts suitable to southern Ontario's climate.

But farmers who want to get out of tobacco won't have an easy time finding a market for crops that are already being hurt by imports. Local markets for more fresh produce are limited and the director of the Simcoe County Horticultural Research Station adds that "there's not a hope in hell of tobacco growers getting acreage contracts with companies [to grow] process[ing] vegetables."[43] In short, a tobacco farmer who gets out of the business and tries to switch to vegetable crops will have to face the same pressure from world-market prices as any other cash-crop farmer. Zimmer told me, "We can produce the products if the Ministry of Agriculture and Food will guarantee us the markets; if they will guarantee, for example, that they won't import strawberries right when our crop is coming off."[44]

In late 1984 Canadian growers got still more bad news when President Reagan asked the US International Trade Commission to investigate tobacco imports from Canada and other countries; the US plans to impose import restrictions.[45] Understandably, Ontario's tobacco growers are worried about the future and have decided that they never want to see another year like 1984. Because of their intensive political lobbying, it is now likely that these growers will have their business regulated by a national Tobacco Marketing Board with supply-management powers. In the fall of 1984, the House of Commons passed legislation to allow the Board to be formed.[46] Because the General Agreement on Tariffs and Trade (GATT) allows countries with supply-management to control imports, tobacco farmers would also be able to be protected from any future imports of low-priced tobacco.

This solution points to another moral quandary. Supply-management marketing boards work to develop new markets and to encourage the use of their commodities. If this new board is set up, the federal government will solve the economic injustice done to tobacco farmers by cutting out cheap imports from multinationals. But it will also extend the life

of a failing industry that makes people ill; even multinationals with investments in tobacco companies are diver-
sifying their business holdings because they know the tobacco
industry is in trouble.[47] Cigarette smoking is gradually declining in Canada; in 1985, the manufacturers' demand for
flue-cured tobacco dropped once again. Farmers were upset
the previous year because they sold 170 million pounds; this
year, farmers will only be able to sell 135 million pounds,
while manufacturers bring in cheaper imports from Brazil,
Zimbabwe, Argentina and Malawi.[48]

The federal government has two choices. It can decide to
get out of the tobacco business and into the business of
helping farmers choose alternate crops: if it takes this route,
it will have to make the political effort to curb produce
imports from the US so that Canadian farmers will be able to
supply their own local markets. Or it can go ahead with its
plan to prop up the tobacco industry with a marketing
board, which also allows the federal government to keep a
lucrative source of tax income. In 1984, Ontario's provincial
government apparently supported this view; once the tobacco
uproar had slipped out of the headlines, the government
and four cigarette companies quietly slipped a subsidy to the
two thousand tobacco growers who were hurt when the
manufacturers cut back demand. The four major cigarette
companies ended up giving an $11 million subsidy to the
growers, while the provincial cabinet added an additional
$1.7 million to the pot.[49]

"My uncle died of cancer," Hugh Zimmer said, looking
at me intently. "It's a bit like the people who make nuclear
weapons. Really, I'm in the same position." He is not alone;
whether or not they will admit it, politicians also share some
responsibility for the tobacco grower's dilemma. If we were
to insist on tighter import restrictions on fresh produce
along with better prices for our locally-grown crops, there
might be incentive for tobacco growers to grow other farm
products. But for all its health hazards, tobacco is just too
rewarding for the government to lose as a taxable crop.

The import policies of governments and multinationals
raise many different issues for farmers. However little we
may know about agriculture, most of us can sympathise with

farmers' concerns because the crops and livestock they produce are essential for our well-being. But some of Canada's most prosperous farmers make a fairly comfortable living growing a crop which is controversial because it is known to cause illness. Ontario's tobacco farmers have found themselves caught in the middle of two serious issues. The first of these issues we can see clearly; it concerns the promotion of a product which creates medical costs for the taxpayer, not to mention serious illness, and in many cases, death. And while even staunch opponents of the tobacco industry are reluctant to blame the farmer for the problem, one authority states that the average tobacco farm in Canada is indirectly responsible for ten Canadian deaths each year.[50] A recent study shows that while Canadians spent two billion dollars on tobacco products in 1979, the taxpayer also spent five billion dollars to cover health care and related costs for people with tobacco-related illnesses.[51] While it is easy to care about the livelihood of the farmer who grows tomatoes or grapes, it is a little less easy to convince many people that we should pay a tax to subsidise an industry that damages people's health.

7
Corporate Agribusiness and the Cheap Food Policy

Usually we see farmers and bankers as adversaries: their frequent conflicts lead to personal tragedy and headline news. But the corporate agribusiness community—traders, processors, wholesalers and retailers—have a different way of looking at agriculture. They implicitly see the farmer as a bottom-rung supplier of cheap raw materials for industry, much as one might see the ore extracted from a mine in terms of its dollar value as a finished car or household appliance. There is a growing body of evidence to support the view that food-related corporations see real food profits in terms of the extra revenues generated from the processing and retailing of the finished product.[1] From this vantage-point, farming as a business, a social structure or a way of life means little unless its products can raise profits through these "value-added" aspects of the food industry. If the farm cannot provide the cheap raw material for this industry, it has to shut down, just as a mine does when it's no longer profitable to extract its ore. The fact that these disappearing "inefficient" farms happen to produce our food supply may not count for much in the corporate profit picture. And if this really is the case, it becomes easier to understand why Canadian farmers cannot get fair prices for their products; it may be more profitable for corporations either to seek out the cheapest possible commodities on the world market or to grow those products on their own factory-farms in countries where labour is cheap.

Large corporations can also have a hidden effect on the price the farmer gets for food through speculative trade on the commodity futures markets. The major North American markets are located in the United States; they include the Chicago Board of Trade, which sells contracts in wheat, soybeans, corn and oats, the Minneapolis and Kansas City grain markets, and the Chicago Mercantile Exchange, which deals in cattle, live hogs and pork bellies. Because of their huge volume of trade, these markets set the price trends for the continent, and often for the world. Canada has one major futures market, the Winnipeg Commodity Exchange, which trades contracts in barley, oats, rye, rapeseed and flaxseed. Only grains used for livestock feed may be sold on the futures market; in Canada, the sale of wheat for human consumption is controlled by the Wheat Board, which buys all the farmers' grain for export sales. It is worth mentioning that western farmers fought to establish both the Board and the prairie Wheat Pools in order to stop the price swings in the futures markets during the Depression.[2].

The futures markets may seem remote to most of us since they deal not in tangible goods, but in pieces of paper which bear the promise to buy or sell a certain amount of a commodity at a specified price and future date. A trader rarely takes delivery of real goods. Instead, he may decide to pay a low price for a contract in January which allows him to acquire a certain volume of grain in March. If grain prices rise, his contract increases in value and he can sell it just before it expires and make a profit. On the other hand, a speculator can also enter the market and sell a contract for a quantity of grain, anticipating that prices will start to fall soon. When prices decline as far as he thinks they will go, he can re-purchase the contract and make a profit.[3]

Traders also "hedge" on the market; a miller, for example, may plan to buy grain on the cash market at a future date when he needs to make flour for his customers. But he may expect to pay a low price, only to find that grain shortages have pushed the price up when he gets around to buying it. In order to prevent the financial loss that could result, the miller can also buy a futures contract for the grain; if the price of grain goes up, so does the value of his contract. Now he can sell that piece of paper and use his profits to buy the grain for his mills at the higher-than-expected cash price. But if grain prices had dropped instead, his losses on the futures market would be offset by the purchase of cheap grain and a saving for his business. In a similar way, trading companies can (and do) buy grain from farmers[4] which they will later re-sell to processors. If the cash price for grain stops to drop, the trader will lose money when he sells his purchase. But if he also sells a futures contract for grain while prices are still good, then he can offset any losses that occur when he must re-sell the farmers' grain for cash.[5]

On the face of it, hedging on the futures market can help both farmers and corporate interests to avoid losing money. I have only met one farmer so far who has tried it; those who do generally have more disposable income than most average farmers. But in fact, the markets are dominated by corporate interests which both hedge and speculate. And these corporate speculators are food traders, not food producers; they buy and sell on the futures markets to make a profit for themselves, not for the farmer. Traders insist that without speculation, hedging would be impossible; besides "accepting the risk" which the hedger is unwilling to take, speculators point out that they bring large sums of money into the futures market, making it easier for others to hedge.[6] In fact, the line between hedging and speculation is easily crossed because of the power of trading companies involved in the futures game. Dan Morgan in *Merchants of Grain* points out how the world's major traders began to set up private "futures markets", selling grain among themselves when the US government set limits on futures speculation in the 1970s. At one point, the traders began to invite what Morgan calls "some of the wildest speculators in the world" into their parallel soybeans market, which eventually collapsed under the pressure of intense trading. According to Morgan, this incident allowed the traders to demonstrate their ability to conduct their business out of sight of government regulation and the public eye. And he believes that such "private markets" still exist today, alongside the main exchanges.[7]

While the price the farmer ultimately gets has to be affected by this kind of manipulation, the steps linking the farmer and the speculator are not that easy to trace. While there could be hundreds of daily prices set for grain all over the globe, trading companies have the technology and the global reach to collect price information and to negotiate grain prices around the world. Although it is difficult for any one company to "corner the market", there are only five major trading companies controlling the grain supply which farmers produce and the rest of us eat.[8] Even Canadian farmers who are paid by the Wheat Board find that their fairly stable price situation is ultimately affected by the "world" grain price; the final payment they receive for wheat each year is determined by what the Wheat Board was able to earn in overseas sales.[9] The actual price spread between what the farmer earns for wheat and what the trading companies earn is unknown to us. The cash deals of the big traders—including the Wheat Board—are kept secret, allegedly because of the highly competitive markets for world grain.[10]

Farmers hope for stable prices to keep them in business, but speculators can only make good profits when they either anticipate—or cause—rapid fluctuation in prices. The rule of "selling dear and buying cheap" keeps them moving quickly to buy and sell contracts,[11] while hog and beef farmers wonder why they cannot earn back their costs of production. Red meat producers, who have had more trouble than any other group of farmers in this country, have their price determined by the huge volume of livestock on both the US futures and cash markets. Traders insist that supply and demand alone set prices for the farmer, but it would be naive to stop there. While working for *Radio Noon* I observed that big surges in futures trading were often followed immediately by a jump on retail prices. Remember the winter frosts in Florida's orange groves during the early 1980's? Naturally, the future supply of orange juice can be reduced by bad weather, but these cold snaps had no effect on the large supplies already on hand. That didn't stop retailers from raising the price of juice as the frost made dramatic headlines and futures traded wildly. There may be a legitimate argument for hedging on the futures market, but it is hard to defend the activities of the independent speculator in food prices. After spending time with so many farmers who were trying to make ends meet, I find it very hard to accept the idea that highly-educated gamblers with little personal interest in food production should be part of the system that sets the farmers' price for food. When I think that farmers invest their livelihood in growing food for such a low return, I end up questioning people who profit by betting on the likelihood of wars and famines. But no one claims that the business of food pricing is a moral one and because of this, the speculator will continue to play a large, if shadowy part in it.

There are other, more visible targets for the farmer's concerns about the prices he gets. The power of multi-nationals leads some farmers to worry about the spread of corporate farming in Canada and its effect on prices, par-ticularly in the Maritimes. McCain Foods of New Brunswick is the dominant player in that part of the country, where about one-third of Canada's potato crop is sold to processors and McCain buys over half that amount for use in frozen products.[12]

McCain is a private family company ranking among the top one hundred and fifty in Canada, with over seven hundred million dollars a year in annual sales. The McCain family had a long and well-established reputation in the seed potato trade before they opened their first New Bruns-wick processing plant in 1957.[13] Since then they have grown to fourteen plants in Canada, the US, England, France, the Netherlands, Spain and Australia. Originally, they began operating with their own funds, supplemented by govern-ment bonds and a line of credit at the Bank of Nova Scotia (the company's Chairman, Harrison McCain, now sits on the Board of Directors of that Bank). Both the bank and the provincial government were pleased with their investment; McCain now employs 2,500 people in New Brunswick alone.[14] The firm has also expanded into other areas; it owns another company which makes potato-harvesting equipment, as well as a fertilizer company and a trucking firm which ships McCain products to market.[15] Because of these acquisitions, some local farmers are becoming worried that they might be forced to depend on the company for all their farm inputs, as well as their market.

The McCain group of companies is a vertically integrated multinational; it is also a fairly close-mouthed family operation. A number of farmers have commented that there are few political brakes on this kind of corporate expansion in their province; it may be significant that New Brunswick has no farm land use legislation. It even lacks the more common "food land guidelines" which all provinces without strict farmland laws have now adopted.[16]

Understandably, potato farmers in New Brunswick wanted more clout in dealing with McCain. Low prices are a big problem for these farmers. Since New Brunswick has the second-largest potato crop in the Maritimes (after Prince Edward Island) its farmers were enthusiastic supporters of the proposed Eastern Canada Potato Marketing Agency. That body was supposed to be a central-desk seller of both table and processed potatoes,[17] but the Maritimes, Quebec and Ontario could not come to any final agreement to set it up. Instead, New Brunswick farmers, like their counterparts in Ontario, now have a province-wide potato agency which allows them to negotiate prices collectively with the processors. But many farmers are still concerned about low prices; while corporate buyers such as McCain say little about their financial dealings with farmers, there is small doubt that growers want more price security in their uncertain market. "The market has been in such turmoil for a number of years," an official with the New Brunswick Federation of Agriculture told me. "What would we lose by working toward [a supply-managed board]?"[18]

Many people wanted to see the Eastern Canadian agency work toward a quota system which would help the farmer earn back his costs of production. One of the original negotiators told me that the agency fell through because P.E.I. did not want to restrict its expanding potato market.[19] However, New Brunswick growers apparently liked the idea of an agency which could control production in other provinces to help them get a fair price; also, the agency would have hit hard at corporate control over potato prices. A McCain spokesman told me that his company sets prices in the context of the North American market;[20] this market is, in turn, dominated by massive potato production in the northwestern United States. Again, it is the farmer, not the corporation, who is hurt by fluctuating prices.

Whereas McCain's frozen food business has grown quickly over thirty years, there has been a decline in the amount of farmland planted in potatoes. Between 1971 and 1976, the number of commercial farms growing potatoes dropped from 8,460 to 6,740 — a reduction of 26 percent. Many farmers across the Maritimes have been forced to quit the business because of poor prices, and over the past twenty years, remaining farms have grown larger by buying up those who went out of business. Prince Edward Island is a case in point: by 1978, twenty farmers in P.E.I. controlled one-half of that province's potato acreage.[21] The threat of corporate farm takeovers led P.E.I. to pass legislation in 1982, setting limits on the amount of farmland held by individuals or corporations. The law was designed to preserve the traditional pattern of small land-holdings in the province, addressing the added concern of large farmland ownership by absentee landlords.[22] P.E.I. has six to seven hundred thousand acres of land in farming; the law allows large corporations to own, lease or rent no more than three thousand acres.[23]

I learned more about the problems of agriculture on the Island from J.P. Hendricken, a farmer who runs a mixed operation in Kings County, about twenty miles east of Charlottetown. His diversified farm provides him with enough income to stay in business. Besides potatoes, he raises strawberries, grains, turnips and feeder pigs (he candidly adds that the latter "are worth nothing"). Like New Brunswick, P.E.I. has a home-grown family corporation as a major buyer for processing potatoes. Cavendish Farms is owned by the Irving Family; it is a small but growing company which competes with McCain for the potato and vegetable processing market. A spokesman for the company told me that they now supply fifteen to twenty percent of that market across Canada.[24] While Hendricken himself does not sell to Cavendish, he is actively involved in the National Farmers' Union, which is concerned about that company's pricing policies. As the major buyer in P.E.I., Cavendish negotiates prices with farmers through the processing firms. The P.E.I. Potato Marketing Board has no power to negotiate the price of processed potatoes for the farmers; it deals mainly with the promotion of fresh potatoes only.

Cavendish is not alone in the P.E.I. market; McCain also negotiates individually with farmers who have potatoes to sell.[25] And like McCain, Cavendish also operates a corporate farming business. I have been told by farmers that Cavendish buys and rents land from farmers; Hendricken claims that the company offers the farmer more rent for the use of the land than any small family farmer would be able to pay. When I asked a Cavendish spokesman how much land they owned, I was told rather cautiously, "You know how much we own — it's fairly well known." I didn't, but I did learn that Cavendish grows about 20 percent of the potatoes they process on their own corporate land holdings.[26] Later, an official with the P.E.I., Federation of Agriculture told me that there was some question about Cavendish owning more than the three-thousand acre limit on corporate land holding in the province; he explained that the government Land Use Commission is holding hearings on how to deal with an alleged breach of the limit.[27] Whether it was because of the hearings of not, I was unable to get more hard information on land-holdings in the province, although I certainly heard sharp comments about the extent of corporate influence and the link between government and agriculture. "Governments are puppets of corporate interests," J.P. Hendricken says bluntly. "McCain and Irving *are* the government. It's a Third World country in the Maritimes."

The growers who sell processed potatoes to the larger firms are not the only ones with price problems. Fresh potato prices are very low in P.E.I. which should make sense to shoppers who know that potatoes are about the cheapest vegetable in the supermarket, even with the retail markup. The National Farmers' Union and the Federations of Agriculture in the Maritimes have been lobbying the federal government to include potatoes under the federal crop stabilisation programme. So far, they have been unsuccessful, even with recent changes made in the Stabilisation Act. One P.E.I. farm leader told me that more lobbying may be needed by national farm groups such as the Canadian Federation of Agriculture or the Canadian Horticultural Council.[28] But some farmers, including Hendricken, raise the possibility that corporate interests have worked to prevent it. "It would make the companies look bad," Hendricken added. When I spoke to Cavendish, I was surprised to hear their spokesman comment that there "was no ongoing lobby" for stabilisation in the province,[29] when in fact, the idea is a popular one, supported by every major farm group.

It is not hard to understand why the idea has so much support. Maritime potato growers have a very difficult time meeting their costs of production. Hendricken explained that it costs twelve hundred dollars an acre to produce potatoes—excluding personal costs of living for the farmer and his family. He added that a farmer typically *loses* three hundred dollars an acre, which makes it easy to see why so many have left the business. And as in other parts of Canada, P.E.I. farmers have faced inflated land values along with low food prices; as land values began to drop, many farmers lost their equity and later, their farms. Now much of the land they once owned is standing idle. And in spite of P.E.I.'s land-use legislation, Hendricken has a bleak view of the future. "When the land isn't worth anything, they'll [government] give it to the corporate interests and let them rape it," he remarked.

The Maritimes are no doubt the only area in Canada where corporate buyers have managed to dominate such a large part of the farm economy. In fact, I was told that when McCain moved into New Brunswick, farmers quickly geared themselves up for the processed potato market. And both McCain and Cavendish have created jobs in the processing industry, although their non-union employment policies have been quite controversial.

Did the farmer who suggested the region was a Third World Country have a point? I could see certain parallels myself. In places where poverty and unemployment are the rule, people are susceptible to the lure of a large corporate presence. The Maritimes is no exception. Multinationals

involved in every area of food production have become a
threat to many family farmers who have little say in the
price they get for their crops. In the case of Maritime potato
growers, good prices are only likely if they pull together and
demand a marketing board with supply-management powers.
Unless that happens, even federal crop-stabilisation would
be a temporary solution to a deep-seated problem.

Some farmers are concerned about the power of corporate
farming, but it has not materialised as a major threat to the
family farm in Canada in the way that it has in the United
States. Granted, 1981 census figures show an 18 percent drop
in the number of Canadian family farms over a ten-year
period. About sixty thousand individual family farms went
out of business during that time. There is also a census
category for farms set up as formal partnerships where
legally-binding partnerships are made between parents, children or other relatives on a family farm; this type of operation dropped by almost half over the decade, from over
21,000 farms in 1971 to almost 11,500 farms in 1981. Family
farms that are legally incorporated rose slightly; so did
institutional farms, including co-ops, experimental operations and the holdings of religious communities, such as the
Hutterites. Corporate farms which are owned and financed
by people who do not farm them rose 27 percent over the
decade, from 911 to 1,247. Corporate land-holding was up 18
percent in the census, which amounts to about ten percent of
Canada's total farmland.[30] Because these are 1981 census
figures, they could be misleading; although these are the
most recent ones we have, they were gathered long before the
recent wave of farm bankruptcies and foreclosures, which
will show up in the census of 1991.

Family farms are still the norm in Canada, but there is no
doubt that they are decreasing in number. In many cases,
this simply means that some of the big, prosperous farms just
get bigger. Although corporate farming has increased in
almost all provinces,[31] there is not much evidence that many
Canadian corporations want to be directly involved in
farming. What will continue is the farmers' practice of renting
land from corporate investors who eventually hope to use it

for urban development. It is land which farmers cannot afford to buy. Farmland rental rose thirty percent between 1971 and 1981, while the total amount of land in farming showed a five percent drop over that period.[32] These figures will no doubt rise in the 1991 census.

Meanwhile, many farmers are aware that corporate interests play a big part in the price they pay for food. Farmers deal every day with middlemen—processors, livestock markets or grain elevator operators. But for the rest of us, the most visible evidence of this corporate power comes from our local supermarket.

In Canada we spend less on our food than any other country, with the exception of the United States. But most of what we pay for that food does not go to the farmer. For years, Ontario's largest farm organization, the Ontario Federation of Agriculture (OFA) has monitored the growing spread between the share of the food dollar the farmer gets and the amount that goes to the retail sector of the business. Between 1979 and 1984, this monthly "food basket" showed that the farmers' share dropped from 59¢ to 49¢.[33] The pattern is similar across the country; prairie farmers receive about four dollars a bushel for their wheat, a price which has changed little over the past ten years, while the price of bread has climbed. In fact, of the $40 billion Canadians spent on food in 1982, farmers earned only $12 billion, or thirty percent of the total. Most of the remainder—$23 billion— went to processors, wholesalers and retailers, while food imports accounted for the other five billion dollars spent on food that year.[34] The middleman is doing well in the food business, while the men and women who actually grow the food are feeling the squeeze.

Canadian processors have acquired power over the years by taking over many of the small, family-run processing companies that once operated in Canada. For example, during the 1960s, there were over one hundred tomato processors in Canada, mostly owned by Canadians. Now there are less than fifty. Four of them have the largest share of the market; three of these are US-owned.[35] Between 1968 and 1982, Ontario plants that process table milk dropped from 163 to 35. Now four big firms dominate that sector of

Ontario's food industry—Labatts, Westons, Beatrice Foods and Beckers. And while the price the farmer gets for table milk is controlled through an agreement with the provincial marketing board, Ontario, and British Columbia are the only two provinces that do not exercise any control over the price the processor and the retailer add on to the milk we drink.[36]

Both the vertical integration—and often, the foreign ownership—of Canada's food industry helps corporations set the price of the food we eat. With their buying power, they can purchase cheap food on the world market; they can also get big-volume discounts from wholesalers, many of which are integrated into their own "diversified" retail businesses. For Canada's retail conglomerates, the most common "secondary" activity is wholesaling; retailers also invest in food processing. Perhaps the best-known example is the Weston Group which owns the Loblaws supermarket chain as well as a solid share of Canada's bakery, dairy, fish processing and frozen food businesses. (Weston also has its own foreign subsidiaries).[37] About sixty percent of Canada's retail food sales are made through the large chains. There are eleven major chains; although none of them spans the country, six of them (A & P, Canada Safeway, Dominion, Loblaws, Steinbergs and Provigo) own well over half the supermarkets.[38] Out of the "top six" retailers, over half the operations are foreign-owned—including those stores in the Dominion chain recently sold to the US-owned A & P (a company which, in fact, is owned by a US holding company on behalf of a German conglomerate). Canada Safeway is also foreign-owned.[39] Whereas foreign ownership of Canada's food industry is lower than other sectors of our economy, the foreign ownership of Canadian businesses in general is higher than average for Western countries. And because of this, we have one of the most foreign-dominated food sectors of any industrialized country in the world. Thirty to forty percent of the food processing and retail business in this country is foreign-owned.[40]

Food in Canada is also sold through "independent" grocers who do about forty percent of the retail business. Many of these are franchise operations (IGA, for example), where the proprietor who leases the store earns profits and underwrites the losses; in return for the franchise, he has to accept the firm's brand-name wholesale products at a price determined by the wholesaler.[41]

The links in the retail food chain become more complex when we realize how the corporations that own our local supermarkets are tied in to the wholesale end of the business. It has become fairly common now for corporate food distributors to get produce from the farm gate to the company's chain and independent retail outlets, both at home and in foreign countries. For those of us who are used to thinking of retailers such as Loblaws as places to shop, the corporate food-buying power of these businesses might be worth a closer look. Weston, for example, is a wholesaler for IGA; it also owns the wholesale National Grocers, a firm used by the Atlantic-based Red and White supermarkets and by Ziggys, a specialty-food retailer owned by Loblaws, (which is owned by Weston). Another corporation, the Oshawa Group, owns the Food City chain and wholesales both to them and to IGA.[42] In recent years, so-called "buying groups", have helped retail food chains control their costs—and pay lower prices for food.

Buying groups have been used by smaller retailers and co-ops for years as a way of getting better wholesale prices that would keep them competitive with the larger chains. But some retail buying groups have now become huge, often as large as supermarket chains themselves. In fact, the five largest food retail buying groups are made up of groups of chains. While their massive buying practices have raised the question of monopoly and price-fixing, there is nothing illegal about what they are doing, as long as the wholesalers give all buying groups equal access to the same pricing discounts.[43] Still, Canada's top five buying groups wield considerable power; they account for 85 percent of all retail food sales in this country. The big five include Foodwide (which buys for Loblaws and Provigo), Volume One (the buyer for Dominion and Steinberg) and the IGA-Safeway buying group.[44] Buying-group practices may help the consumer, but farmers no doubt suffer if they feel pressured by wholesalers to take lower prices. A supermarket buying group also looks for the cheapest produce available on the world market; this includes big-volume imports either from countries with cheap labour costs or from the heavily-subsidised farm sector of the EEC. The Canadian farmer must struggle to remain competitive in such a market. Many stay in business only because they specialise for the processed-food trade.

In southwestern Ontario, many tomato and vegetable growers contract crops to large processors at the beginning of the season through their marketing board—which does not have the power to regulate the price or the supply of produce. This arrangement combines the independent family farmer with conditions resembling a factory-farm. The processor who contracts with the farmer will outline the growing conditions of the crop and state the varieties the farmer is to grow, the size of the crop and the chemicals to be used on it.[45] In other words, the management decisions normally made by the farmer are to a large degree made by the processor; in return, the farmer gets a sure buyer for his crop along with all the usual risks involved in growing it.

Although farmers understand that a complex corporate marketing system can hurt their prices, they usually blame their tight incomes on Ottawa's cheap food policy. The specifics of this policy are not easy to grasp; farmers point out that urban shoppers enjoy a constant supply of food at reasonable prices while too often the farmer earns less than what it cost to produce the food. While no official has ever admitted that such a policy exists, farm groups say it is self-evident; politicians have to face an electorate which, for the most part, does not produce its own food. Low food prices at the retail level keep people satisfied and allow politicians to take some credit for the voters' well-being. Meanwhile, the farmer's problems remain invisible; what we see are the retailers and their well-stocked neighbourhood supermarkets. But if it is true that agriculture is at the bottom-end of the "agri-food" system as a supplier of raw materials, then the cheap food policy starts to make sense. Agriculture Canada's major discussion paper on the future of agriculture spells out the role of Canadian farming as a growing partner in an export industry designed to give a boost to Canada's trade and to help our balance of payments.[46]

Brewster Kneen, a Nova Scotia lamb producer, goes further; he argues that Ottawa's cheap food policy allows the food processors and distributors to get cheap labour and raw materials from farmers through a series of public and private subsidies which underwrite the cost of producing food. These public subsidies include capital grants to farmers and provincial stabilization payments, plus hidden costs, such as unemployment benefits, the waste of idle land, social dislocation and growing food dependence on foreign imports — all the result of farmers being forced out of business because of low prices. Kneen adds that there are also private subsidies for cheap food production, among them cheap farm labour (many members of the family work for nothing), off-farm employment to keep the business going, loss of equity as farm debt builds up while the farmer loses money and the depletion of resources, which no doubt includes farmland monocropped year after year to help a farmer make ends meet.[47] Kneen also points out that an explicit cheap food policy includes government permission for Canadian companies to import cheap food from any country which has a "comparative economic advantage" — a euphemism for long growing seasons combined with cheap labour and land, both of which are often provided to multinational corporations by repressive governments.[48]

From this point of view, the real Cheap Food Policy becomes more than a catch-phrase to describe the farmer's economic plight. Kneen writes:

> ...there are few illusions left for farmers. We know we are being relentlessly squeezed so that we either get out, get much bigger and accept the role of managers with "investors" owning the farms, or get smaller and subsidise our food production with off-farm employment, as has been the case for years. It is this privately subsidised farming that has been one of the mainstays of Canada's Cheap Food Policy.[49]

Other farmers look at the Cheap Food Policy somewhat differently, adding that farmers get squeezed because they do, in fact, produce costly food through over-use of chemical fertilizers, pesticides and large farm machinery. Farmers may do this to produce bumper crops that will pay for costly land and otherwise help them break even. Still, it has been suggested by one farmer that food is cheap for Canadians because many of us have high incomes, while farmers themselves have production costs that are too high to be compensated fairly in the marketplace.[50] Tom Oegema, of the Christian Farmers Federation of Ontario, a group which stresses stewardship of the family farm, comments:

> North American agriculture is a high cost agriculture...
> to the millions of people in less-developed parts of
> the world who would love to have the food we grow, but
> can't afford it. Therefore, we should temper our opti-
> mism about exporting ourselves out of our surpluses.
> The technology we employ on our farms is ingenious but
> expensive. It also makes us totally dependent on an
> industrial infrastructure. If we add in the hundreds of
> man-years spent in producing all the technology, pes-
> ticides, fuels, etc. that agriculture uses, then maybe the
> individual farmer in North America isn't nearly as
> efficient as he is cracked up to be.[51]

While it is often said that a farmer feeds at least fifty persons, it now takes the labour of another fifty people to keep that farmer operating today.

Commercial farmers like to think they are independent business people, but they cannot function without the aid of the corporate giants. Multinational companies sell the farmer his supplies; they also buy, process, market and sell the food he produces, often making handsome profits at the farmer's expense. The family farm is still a going concern in Canada. It has to be; corporations stay away from farming because they realise that none of their industrial employees would work for the meagre return most farmers get. From the corporate point of view, farmers are there to provide the "raw material" for eventual corporate profit. Aside from their contribution to the bottom line, farmers are worth nothing to the agribusiness giants.

Part III: Goals and Solutions

8
Networks and Co-ops

There are three hundred thousand farmers in Canada, a country of twenty-five million people. In the political arena, no group that size gets much attention without building alliances with other groups to advance its goals. One positive step Canadian farmers could take on their own behalf would be to build a national constituency of concerned citizens whom they see as political allies and not just as consumers of the products they sell. Usually farmers organise themselves either through provincial and loose national federations or through commodity groups; this helps them define their business interests more clearly.

While farmers need these groups, their agendas often have a fairly narrow focus. For example, the Canadian Federation of Agriculture is a major farm organisation which represents a traditional approach to farm lobbying.[1] The CFA includes representatives from all the provincial Federations of Agriculture, as well as delegates from a number of commodity groups—the Canadian Horticultural Council, the Dairy Farmers of Canada and the three Western wheat pools. While the CFA has considered forming alliances with major business groups, David Kirk, the Federation's Executive Secretary, feels that these links would be too difficult for them to establish. He describes manufacturing, retail and labour organisations as groups which develop broad strategies for economic change which are intended to benefit the country as a whole. "These are the 'big levers,'" says Kirk. "These [groups include] broad-based theories and we would not know which one to choose ideologically." As an example, he pointed out that members of marketing boards might be at odds with food processors if the CFA got involved with the concerns of manufacturers' organisations.

The CFA has not considered the possibility of networking with issue-oriented urban groups. "We are inclined to doubt the practicality of setting up permanent relations or negotiating joint positions [with other groups]," Kirk told me. "We are responsible to our members as they are to theirs." He candidly admits that a large group such as the CFA is not always unanimous in its views on certain issues, making it somewhat difficult to agree which outside groups to support. Nevertheless, they recently made an exception; the CFA has joined the Canadian Coalition on Acid Rain. While the CFA states that this is not their usual practice, the alliance may produce the kind of helpful contacts outside the farm community which can only serve the farmers' interests in the long run.

Another smaller farm organisation goes further in its outside involvement than the CFA. The National Farmers' Union is an 8,000-member organisation, with most of its strength in western Canada. It is known as an outspoken group, somewhat to the left of most farm organisations. Membership is open to family farmers, while commodity groups are not admitted, which plays down the more usual emphasis on the farmer's ties with big business. The NFU's president, Wayne Easter, says "We believe in the concept of Canada—we are one of the few farm groups who do. We are bound together as Canadians...we ignore provincial boundaries and commodity lines. Many farm groups are rubber stamps for government and over time, their policies make close connections with them."[2] This philosophy has attracted the farmers who work hardest for the organisation; it has also kept the more conservative farmers away.

"There is a certain philosophy," Easter continues, "not just that farmers benefit, but that we build a better society." The NFU, for example, may criticise high interest rates, but it takes a more comprehensive view of the problem; it will also consider the possibility that lower interest rates could help well-off farmers swallow up smaller operators. Because of the focus on broader social issues that relate to farming, the NFU is more receptive to concerns which also interest people off the farm. "But this can cause extreme difficulty," says Easter. "People join, but they may take issue with our views, for example, against the arms race." In 1984, the NFU endorsed the nationwide Peace Petition Caravan campaign; their Policy Statement that year included support for issues as diverse as homemakers' pensions and universal medical care.[3] The NFU has had trouble building the organisation east of the Rockies; Ontario membership is down, and there are no members at all in Quebec. Some of this has to do with its adamant position on the issue of supply-management for red meat, a stand which angers many more conservative farmers, especially in Ontario. Still the NFU is unusual because it insists on placing farm problems in a broader social context.

A political alliance between farm organisations and the labour movement would be a sensible place to start building the farm constituency. The support would be mutually beneficial; farmers often point out that good farm-gate prices stimulate jobs in the city, while more jobs mean more money to pay the farmer for food. Unions have organising expertise that could benefit farmers in their dialogue with the public. But there is a catch. Farmers who see themselves as business people often try to distance themselves from labour unions; some farm organisations fear and dislike labour militancy. Several years ago, at the annual meeting of an Ontario farm group, delegates debated how they ought to protest the failure of the provincial government to halt the spread of farm bankruptcies. The suggestions on the floor included a proposal for a march on the provincial legislature. The idea was turned down because it was considered "too radical". During the discussion, a number of farmers remarked that a demonstration would make them look too confrontational, "just like trade unionists."

In fairness to these farmers, it helps to point out that a generation of Conservative government in Ontario set the rules of the game for lodging grievances of this kind. While the Conservatives were in power, the normal route for farm leaders was to set up private meetings with cabinet ministers and other officials to air their views. Invariably, these meetings were set up after farm groups staged a media blitz to embarrass politicians who made a blunder. With this ritual firmly in place, public displays of protest received relatively little support from Ontario's farmers, with one recent exception to the rule which may signal a change. In July, 1985, the Ontario Federation of Agriculture marshalled two thousand farmer-members in front of the provincial legislature to protest the new Liberal government's lack of action on farm economic problems. At the same time, groups of farmers lobbied urban MPPs in an effort to make them more aware of the farmer's concerns. But the old "protester" stigma is still there. The OFA's leader described the day's activities as "not a demonstration against the government, but a rally in support of farmers."[4]

While there is no hard evidence to show that most farmers dislike union-style protest tactics, I have heard farmers in other provinces complain that organised labour has hurt their business directly. Farmers have often told me that the high wage demands of union members push up the cost of doing business for food processors and retailers. As a result, the retail cost of food goes up and the consumer thinks that the farmer must be doing well. "We've got to put the hammer on those [union] guys," one prosperous beef producer in Ontario told me. Yet a federal government study on food-price rises during the period of high inflation between 1970 and 1982 shows that food prices rose 214 percent during that time. Meanwhile, labour costs in both food processing and retailing accounted for a total of 18.3 percent of the jump—an amount considered small by the authors of the study.[5]

Occasionally, farmers and union members work together. In 1982, a local of the United Auto Workers became involved with the beleaguered farmers of Bruce County, Ontario in their protests against a local bank. The Canadian Labour Congress has also expressed its support for the goals of the Canadian Farm Survival Association, a controversial group whose members have staged peaceful sit-ins to prevent bailiffs from foreclosing family farms.[6] Many farmers question the use of these "direct-action" tactics; whether or not they are justified is a separate issue. The farmers involved were willing to work with union members because they saw themselves, not as business people, but as poorly-paid and organised workers. Some farm organisations understand this view. While they do not support the Farm Survivalists' approach, the National Farmers' Union often takes fairly blunt views on the treatment of the farmer. President Wayne Easter insists that "you cannot always be Mr. Nice Guy... exploitation is now very sophisticated. Slavery was once very visible. Today we have economic slavery; the home is mortgaged to the bank. It all amounts to the same thing as physical slavery. Government has the power to prevent that from happening."[7]

Is the farmer an exploited worker? A Toronto newspaper recently printed this letter from a farmer who no doubt speaks for many others:

> Over the years, every section of our working class has been exploited by the rich. Gradually, the working class became organised and fought back with unions and human rights and equal rights. Farmers are the last frontier for the rich; we are not organised and have absolutely no protection. We don't have cost of living allowance, hospital plans, dental plans, holidays or any of the frills most people have now. A farmer does not go on strike or make ridiculous demands; he's quite satisfied with almost anything. He doesn't have sick leave or days off or pension plans or workers' compensation or even unemployment insurance. He works seven days a week. Even when injured or sick, his days average out to 12 hours and he earns about 25 cents an hour . . . Why can't a farmer be treated with respect and gratitude for producing food for all the experts who suddenly know all the answers? Are we guilty of something I don't know about? . . . [8]

Everything the letter says is true. Over the years that I worked as an agricultural broadcaster, I heard many stories like this one, and it always puzzled me that farmers so seldom protest their plight, in ways that would draw on the support of other citizens. As I traveled across Canada, I met a number of astute farmers who commented that it was difficult to get many farmers to work together until they were all in danger of going broke. "Farmers aren't joiners," one beef producer told me. "If you get more than three together, that would be terrific." His wife added, "In a factory, a worker would be approached by a union organiser who would say, 'join up and we'll help you; membership is ten dollars.' If you do that to a farmer, he would say, 'I just don't have the ten dollars.' "

Like the rest of us, farmers don't like to make public statements about their financial problems in any forum larger than a local meeting—if they go that far. Often they fear reprisals from their banks: I was told that public organising or protest would be noticed, and could mean the refusal of a badly-needed farm loan. Under these conditions, farmers obviously need help and support from urban organisations. Farmers live in relative isolation; people who work alone most of the time have many long hours to worry about financial pressures. For some of these farmers, it must be very hard to realise that there could be any political networking to draw rural and urban interest groups closer together.

The United Church, for example, already has a Standing Committee on Agriculture and Food Resources, a group which prepares study materials encouraging church members to get involved in farm issues. The strategy of building links among groups produces a bloc of supporters in every segment of society; this is one of the reasons why issues such as environmental pollution or fair pay for women get constant media attention. Farm groups could benefit from this kind of networking; they deal with many issues which have a broad enough moral and political focus to interest the urban activist. These include the preservation of foodland, the development of alternative styles of agriculture and a just price for food. This process might also draw more farm groups into lending their support for social concerns off the farm.

There are some hopeful signs that the farm community is beginning to move in new directions. In the Maritimes, a new organisation called the Nutrition Policy Institute wants to draw farmers and urban people together in an effort to form a coherent national food policy. Such a policy would address both the problems of the farmer and the appropriate role for Canada's agriculture in the world context. Brewster Kneen, the Nova Scotia lamb farmer who started the group, points out that most of the studies on farmers' problems do not address the elements in the economic system which create the problems in the first place. "In place of an industrial agricultural policy that produces malnutrition and poverty," he writes, "we wish to develop a nutrition policy committed to providing nourishment and health both for the land and for the people."[9] He reports that the Institute has received a good response so far "from Gander to Alberta;" a support group in Ontario hopes to form a non-profit corporation to assist them with funding. While their initial activities center on research and the preparation of reports, the NPI wants to hold seminars and workshops for public education. They are eager to co-operate and share ideas with individuals who do not normally network with farmers—specifically, people who are professionally concerned with nutrition, such as doctors or other medical workers.[10]

The Saskatchewan Women's Agricultural Network began in February 1985, when the University of Saskatchewan held a conference for rural women, invited to share their concerns as farmers. Later, they had the opportunity to exchange views informally with representatives of urban womens' groups, who were also holding meetings in the area. From this beginning, farm and city women in Saskatchewan are starting to learn more about social issues which affect both groups, including women's property rights in marriage and divorce. By meeting each other on common ground, these women hope to expand into more regional concerns. The network's organiser, Glenis Joyce, told me that "most Saskatchewan people are from small towns and this really helps the discussion along . . . there are some really vibrant women from rural Saskatchewan," she adds, who are getting involved in networking with women in the city.[11]

While both of these groups are just beginning, they point to a new direction for the farm community, one which is bound to help farmers create a much broader constituency. In the meantime, many farmers need to know what they can do right now to solve their financial problems. Farmers who are willing to work together to keep their businesses solvent can try an alternate style of farm management to reduce capital and input costs. When I went to Saskatchewan, I spent some time visiting a family farm co-operative near Fillmore, an hour's drive southeast of Regina on Highway 33. One of the farmers, Keith Wiggins, spoke modestly about a very old idea which has helped him stay in farming. His family and four others farm co-operatively; they own their land in common as well as their machinery. In 1976, they were incorporated as a co-op; their production decisions are made collectively and the families share in the profits. Some of the advantages of this setup are obvious; there is a big drop in the initial costs of farming. Wiggins put it simply: "You don't need five combines. You just need one." In fact, when they got started, they unloaded $65,000 worth of excess machinery at a farm auction. They have a total of six and three-quarters sections of land—well over four thousand acres. They plant grain on 2800 acres and have a hog operation with one hundred breeding sows and another one hundred head of beef cattle.

Keith Wiggins has been farming for thirty years; he bought his own farm in 1948. While the co-operative has been able to work around some of the high costs of farming, there isn't much they can do about the low prices they get for red meat and grain. "And feed grain (for livestock) costs a lot more than I'd like to admit," he says. Still, I was surprised to find that this relatively secure farmer wants to see the system of supply-management set up in the red meat industry. He explained to me that "more than half the people who have beef in Saskatchewan favour the system, but the organisations which represent beef producers don't. They are the rancher types," he added with emphasis. "Independent individualists." He told me that over the past ten years, farmers "have not made a cent" producing beef. For that matter, grain prices are low, too, but the world market price is beyond the farmer's control. Although their operation is surviving financially, they still have to go to the bank and borrow money, "and we are not immune to interest costs."

While his own farm is relatively large, it is run as a co-operative venture and not as a farm factory. Wiggins feels strongly that massive farms are not necessarily the most economically viable. "They say you only survive if you are big," he said, "but they're getting too big. There is an optimum size for farms, and beyond that, I believe your efficiency stops; it starts turning around. Then they're not farmers anymore." I was curious about that statement and I asked him what he felt a farmer was. There was a long pause, as if he was quite stuck for an answer. Finally he said rather thoughtfully, "a farmer has to be contributing part of the labour—and controlling the rest of it."

Before my visit to the Wiggins farm, I had not met other farmers who worked co-operatively. In fact, I was so unfamiliar with the co-op concept that Wiggins had to tell me what it meant. But he didn't talk about the philosophy of co-ops; he paid more attention to the practical details of their successes and the problems they still face. Even the idea of supply-management—an emotional issue for most farmers—got a matter-of-fact nod from him, as though this kind of business co-operation ought to be taken for granted. Later, I wondered why this casual acceptance of farmers working together was something I had never encountered before. For most farmers, a farm is not only a business, but an *independent* business. The irony is that the highly mechanised farmer is completely dependent on unstable world markets, fluctuating interest rates and the pricing policies of multinational corporations. As long as this is the case, farmers can help themselves by becoming a little more "dependent" on the help and partnership of other farmers who face the same problems.

Not every farmer would want to set up a communal business, but there are other alternatives. A group of sheep producers in Nova Scotia's Pictou County have formed a highly successful lamb marketing co-op called Northumberlamb.[12] Since its beginning in 1982, 110 farmers have joined the co-op, which ships fresh lamb to market. The volume of sales has grown steadily along with the membership and one of Northumberlamb's major problems involves keeping ahead of the demand for fresh lamb. While the type of co-op is not new, this particular one has accomplished something out of the ordinary by setting up a central-desk selling system for three-quarters of Nova Scotia's fresh lamb—a *de facto* marketing board, owned and run completely by farmers. The co-op hopes to extend the central-desk system throughout the Maritimes; their aim is to replace imported lamb in the region and in doing this, to encourage local production of lamb, while helping the farmer to get prices that cover his costs. Farmers who want to join Northumberlamb pay a membership fee, but there are no co-op shares or dividends. With the costs down, the difference between what they pay the farmer for lamb and what the lamb sells for on the market is as small as possible. The co-op organisers also try to match the lamb supply to the demand; their lamb-marketing year starts in early spring, when farmers give them an estimate of the amount of lamb they expect to have on hand and when it will be ready for slaughter. With a list of market dates, the co-op can then co-ordinate the lamb supply to match their customers' advance orders. The co-op sets the price every week; all farmers get the same price in any given week, and all co-op customers pay the same price when it is set each week.[13]

Using this approach, the Northumberlamb Co-op has found a practical solution to a marketing problem which has plagued Canada's few lamb producers.

Groups such as Northumberlamb are a badly-needed reminder that farmers who want fair marketing and good prices can get them if they are willing to work together to develop their market. The farmers in Northumberlamb are politically astute enough to realise that by owning and operating their own selling desk, they are more likely to get a fair price. Also, they have managed to eliminate the promotional checkoff, a common cost in many provincial marketing boards which allows these bodies to deduct a percentage of each farmer's cheque for product advertising.

If the idea of co-op farming isn't for everyone, it offers a striking example of what can happen when farmers take the initiative to make their business work. Equally impressive are the efforts of organic farmers who have tackled their economic problems by cutting input costs and developing a specialised market. Even if these are partial solutions, they still boost the morale of farmers who need to feel that they have the power to make things change. Rural co-operation and urban networking will force the farmer to come to grips with the delusion that his real allies are governments and corporate agribusiness. Otherwise, farmers will continue to send us a double message: they want help without basic changes that would rock the corporate boat. The constructive political alternative is a farmers' alliance with urban people and with each other. It is, at least, a solid first step.

9
Organic Farming: A Way Out?

Over the past forty years, most of us have gradually gotten used to the idea that farmers can only provide us with food if they use chemical fertilizers and pesticides. While this is a relatively new way of thinking, it has caught on quickly because of the success farmers have had using chemicals to increase crop yields. Most of us have learned to connect the use of chemicals with the practice of up-to-date agriculture in general, including the use of specialised equipment and improved seed varieties. And because we make this connection so readily, farmers and other business people who support the use of chemicals are seldom questioned when they accuse organic farmers of rejecting modern technology. In my own discussion with conventional farmers, I have often heard this point of view supported by an almost irresistible moral argument: organic farmers who "return to the past" are naive and selfish people who hurt society and even cause starvation by exposing our food supply to the damage of pests and disease.

That would no doubt be the case if farmers tried to remove chemicals from today's industrialised farm operations, where the practice of monocropping has become the farmer's means of survival. Within such a farm system, it becomes almost impossible to do without chemicals; soils that are overworked from the intensive farming of a single crop cannot provide the nutrients that help make crops resistant to disease. But the soil rebuilding and crop rotation techniques used by organic farmers question the idea that a modern, commercially successful farm business must "mass-produce" crops and livestock with the techniques of large-scale industry. Instead, commercial farmers who use organic techniques can produce good crop yields of healthy, disease-free produce. And the case for organic farming has been strengthened by the fact that it offers one way out of the economic difficulties farmers face; it allows them to reduce their operating costs while upgrading the quality of their soil.

There are about two to three hundred commercial organic farms in Canada[1] — a very small percentage of Canada's three hundred thousand farmers. And while they share many practices in common, the term "organic" farming is an ambiguous one. In Quebec, farmers describe what they are doing as *agriculture biologique*,[2] to distinguish it from the practice of farming with chemicals. But whatever term they use to describe themselves, all organic farmers begin with the idea that healthy crops are the result of a well-nourished and properly cultivated soil which is, in turn, our basic food-producing resource. The elimination of pesticides is only one part of their approach to farming. They concentrate most of their attention on soil improvement; often they will add organic matter to their soil, in the form of composted residues of plant material and animal excretions which break down to form the rich, dark soil known as humus. This material nourishes crops; it also feeds soil micro-organisms and earthworms which, in turn, add more organic material to the soil.[3] A handful of this rich, porous soil will crumble easily in the fingers; it holds water well and allows new seedlings to emerge quickly. Some farmers put added nutrients into the soil by planting "green manures" — fields of nitrogen-rich crops such as clover or alfalfa which are then plowed back into the soil. This technique also prevents soil erosion: until they are plowed under, these plants hold soil in place and act as a buffer against wind and rain.[4] Over time, such consistent feeding of the soil assures the farmer that well-tended fields will remain productive for the next generation to work his land. While soil nutrition has been basic to agriculture from the beginning, we may be the first generation to have to re-learn the simple rule-of-thumb that asks farmers to put back what they take out of the soil. Instead, farmers are now taught in ag school to think about the soil as a medium to hold the plant upright so that it can receive nutrition from chemical fertilizers.

Not all farmers accept this view anymore. In the lush orchards of the Okanagan Valley, there are a number of farmers who depend on soil nutrition to give them healthy crops. One of these farmers is Otto Rothe, a slender, gray-haired man. Both he and his wife, Sophia are from Germany; they have been farming in the Okanagan for twenty years, after coming from Edmonton where Otto worked as a carpenter. They cultivate thirty acres of land, producing apples, peaches, apricots and plums, as well as some produce and poultry for their own use. Otto Rothe studied agriculture in Germany and his training included both the standard pruning skills of the orchardist and a technique known as "biodynamic" farming. A quick look around the Rothe farm gives the clue to the technique. Sitting between their house and vegetable garden is the biggest compost pile I have ever seen. It contains about two tonnes of decomposing matter, including produce leftovers, hay, and cow and turkey manure. The pile is shaped like a giant pitchfork, forming a large, composted "U" with two more rows of material down the centre. Even though it includes a lot of manure, there is no odor; there is good air circulation in the pile because of the layers of hay. It takes anywhere from six months to two years for the organic matter in the pile to break down into a rich, fertile loam full of soil nutrients and beneficial micro-organisms.

Otto is enthusiastic about this effort. Grabbing a pitch-fork, he leapt up on the pile and dug into it to show me a black soil rich with earthworms. Curious and a little less daunted by all the rotting material, I climbed up on the pile to have a look around at its expanse of hay and brown plant stalks. We ended up having a lengthy discussion on top of the pile as Otto explained how it fit into his farming operation. He uses ten tonnes of compost per acre a year as a natural fertilizer for his orchard. (Most farmers who use compost use less — up to fifteen tonnes an acre every three years). He doesn't use chemical fertilizers or pesticides; like many organic farmers, he believes that promoting healthy soil is the first step to an abundant, disease-free crop. "You have to have a certain philosophy to farm like this," Otto said. "It takes hard work and dedication. Our endeavour is to bring life into the soil. And we see the soil as an organism," he continued, "just as the earth is an organism. You have to feed the organism in an acre of good soil, just as you have to feed a cow. This allows the root systems of your trees to enlarge, and so the plant's capacity to use the nutrients in the soil becomes bigger." Rothe believes that the presence of certain insects is sometimes the result of chemical imbalances in the soil; he sees composting as one way of correcting soil problems. "Fighting bugs is a negative approach," he says. "The bugs are there to help decompose matter. Even bees do that with flowers; they go after the scent before the flower dies and then they spread it around."

It is difficult to run an orchard without pesticides unless a farmer is willing to put this kind of effort into soil development. But I was told that farmers who raise field crops can use other techniques to keep their produce free of insects and disease. They avoid growing the same crop in the same fields year after year, pointing out that this not only depletes the soil, but also allows pests to lay their eggs in the ground, only to re-emerge the following year to attack that crop.[5] For example, corn is a money-making crop for farmers who often grow it continuously; in order to get a good yield each season, they have to "feed" it with heavy doses of anhydrous ammonia fertilizer. The pesticide Atrazine must also be used, but it is toxic to other crops; if a farmer stops growing corn, the pesticide residues in the soil will make it impossible to plant another crop for several years.[6] To prevent these problems, organic farmers usually set up a system of crop rotations in a mixed-farm setting. As they do this, they often improve cropland that may have been left in very poor condition.

Several mixed organic farms are now well-established in the Eastern Townships of Quebec, in the area about an hour's drive southeast of Lennoxville. It is beautiful country, but the rolling hills look better suited to pastureland than to raising crops, and there are many dairy farms along the country roads. Just south of Scotstown off Highway 257, Bart Hall-Beyer and Monique Scholtz farm fifty-three hectares of land. They run the farm as a legal partnership; Bart's wife, Myrka has a financial investment in the business, but makes her living as a naturalist. The farm produces hogs, poultry, cattle, vegetables, and grain; their small orchard will soon come into production. The four-year old farm is breaking even financially; the farm owners are careful managers who had studied and practiced farming before they went into business. As a student, Monique was interested in ecological farming and was surprised to find that it was taught only "for three hours out of a 45-hour veggie course" she took as part of her programme at McGill University. The farm is a well-organised and businesslike operation which has not escaped the notice of its neighbours. The farmers get healthy crops of winter rye and barley and they joke about the compliments they get from their neighbours, who ask, "What did you spray on them to get them to grow like that?"

Behind their success lies an idea about farming strikingly different from what most farms now live by. "You have to talk about a farm as a living organism," says Bart. He explains that every aspect of the operation is part of a closed system which recycles nutrients and waste products to create new crops and feed livestock. Like many organic farmers, he saves manure from livestock, which is composted with other organic waste products and fed back into the soil. By contrast, the operator of a conventional farm may run a one or two-crop "factory" or a large livestock feedlot. In the case of field crops, chemical fertilizers have to be purchased off the farm since there is no livestock to provide manure. Hog operations or cattle feedlots have the opposite problem; the manure runoff can be so large that it can pollute nearby streams and lakes—along with the farm chemicals leaching out of the soil. Of course, many conventional livestock farmers also raise their own feed; some of them are now using manure on their fields to avoid the high costs of chemical fertilizers. But in general, today's conventional farm faces a tricky moral issue which organic farmers are trying to resolve. Like an urban industrial plant, farms buy and consume energy, while producing waste products and pollution . . . along with a steady supply of food which we can't do without. Organic farmers try to solve the dilemma by recycling as many of their waste products as possible in the operation of the farm.

While the approach may seem old-fashioned to some, there is no longer much doubt that it works. The case for a more "sustainable" style of agriculture got strong public support in 1980 when the United States Department of Agriculture released a major study on organic farming. It viewed "sustainable" farming as the practice of long-term soil improvement techniques, used to produce healthy crops without the use of chemical fertilizers or pesticides. The report documented the commercial success of these farms and praised their techniques of weed and pest control. It also recommended further research in these techniques. But the report made it very clear that today's organic farmer is not trying to return to the agriculture of the 1930's.[7] It is a point that needs repeating, because these farmers still suffer from a "hippie" back-to-the-land image. They do not reject modern farm machinery, but organic farmers are more likely to think that the use of technology has limits.

Farm machinery is costly for every farmer, but if chosen sensibly it should pay for itself, whatever the style of farming. It doesn't always work out that way, and Al Sheresky, an organic grain grower, thinks he knows why. He farms a section of land in Glen Ewan, a good two-hour drive southeast of Fillmore, Saskatchewan and only a few miles from the Manitoba border to the east. He also runs one of Canada's few milling operations for organically-grown grain, for which he has developed a small but loyal group of customers. His own grain production includes wheat, oats, barley, flax and millet. Sheresky is a tall, slim, almost ascetic-looking man, who started his milling business ten years ago and even though the market for his products is a limited one, he manages to break even, doing most of the hard work himself, with the help of his son.

Al Sheresky is convinced that farmers in his area overwork the land and spend far too much money on chemicals. He explained to me that each year, most farmers pay about $37 an acre for chemicals, whereas he only has to pay out $60 over a three-year period to buy seed. "Above and beyond the business of all these inputs," he says, "for many farmers, it just involves the desire to beat John Doe. Machinery is a big factor in this. Why do you need a one-hundred thousand dollar four-wheel drive tractor? You see so many young people who want it all—a big house, a new car,—and they wind up in debt up to their necks. I don't borrow unless I really need to. If I can't afford it, I go without. I never borrow for seed or gas or anything. My Dad never did and I don't intend to."

Sheresky also asks out loud if people get much pleasure and satisfaction out of their farm work anymore, or if they even know how to enjoy it in a mechanised setting. "You can be six feet off the ground in the tractor cab, and the kids even do their work with their headsets on," he said, a little sadly. "So then they don't see—or hear." Sheresky does his own repairs on his farm machinery and he thinks it is unfortunate that many younger farmers don't know how to repair their expensive state-of-the-art machines when they break down. It seems strange to him that a farmer should have to call the manufacturer to fix a bearing because his machine is under warranty. That can get expensive, and Sheresky wonders if the kind of high-input intensive farming that most farmers do today really equips them with the kind of everyday mechanical skills that can save them money in the long run.

Most organic farmers are not philosophically opposed to the use of farm machinery, although you will occasionally find a farmer who chooses horse power to operate his equipment. There are still some sound reasons for farming with horses; often they are used to plow some lower-grade hilly areas which would be difficult to farm mechanically, and which might otherwise not be farmed. In western Ontario, the young president of the Huron County Federation of

Agriculture farms 65 acres of Class Four land with horses and an intriguing collection of ancient farm equipment. Tony and Fran McQuail bought their one-hundred-acre farm in 1973 and they gradually built up a full-time profit-making business by doing off-farm jobs and hard physical work. Eventually, they completed building a solar home and a large barn. Tony explains that it is hard to work with horses, but he finds that they are less likely to damage his soil, which tends to hold moisture. He does all his work with horse-drawn machinery. Unlike tractors, horses reproduce themselves and create fertilizer.

Tony's machinery costs are negligible: he paid one dollar for his hay binder at a farm auction. The binder is a large machine with a wooden reel in front and a blade and a set of tines on the user's left to catch the hay and cut it. The reel then pulls the hay back onto a pair of canvas baffles, where a set of gears lifts it up to what looks like a giant sewing bobbin that spews out twine to bind the hay. It would not be everyone's idea of 1980's harvesting equipment, but it represents a mode of small-scale technology that can work for the farmer who wants to try it. Why should a farmer go through all the hassle? Tony McQuail decided to do it because his interest in environmental concerns has led him to feel that heavily mechanised farming wastes resources and energy. "More labour goes into the farmer's inputs that he himself puts in," he says adamantly.

Whatever the level of technology organic farmers decide to use, all of them have specific reasons for their style of farming. Often, farmers become allergic to chemicals; they are suspicious about long-range health effects. It takes about ten years of thorough testing before a farm chemical gets on the market in Canada, but the confidence some farmers had in the safety of chemicals was shaken by a drug-testing scandal that came to light in 1976 when the US government found that a US firm had falsified tests on a wide range of pesticides and other chemicals. Over one hundred compounds used in Canada were tested by Industrial Biotest Laboratories of Illinois which issued fake results. The tests were commissioned by US chemical companies for the licensing of their product in Canada and many of the tests had to be run once again in both countries to make sure the products were safe. But even so, the chemicals remained on the market, causing one expert to remark that the public were being used as guinea pigs.[8] Many farmers have put safety concerns aside because they feel they cannot afford to farm without these chemicals, but George and Anna Zebroff chose instead to become self-sufficient organic farmers. They live just outside Cawston, a small town on the way into the Okanagan Valley in British Columbia. Their farm is located on the "bench," as local people call the roads that run along the sides of mountains, and the tiny eleven-acre plot produces fruit from a thousand trees, vegetables, honey, lambs, pigs and other small livestock and milk from the family cow. Their production is substantial and they are able to feed themselves and sell the rest of their produce.

George was raised as a member of the Doukhobours, the Russian religious sect once known for the controversial protests of some of its members against government authority. His wife, Anna, recently came here from Czechoslovakia. As we talked about their farm, I learned more about why they had been farming for the past eleven years. "We wanted our kids to be able to eat a blade of grass," George said tersely. "And we wanted to do something with our own little corner to make it clean." The family has no food bills and they grow the kind of fruit that makes you realise what real plums are supposed to taste like. Zebroff is not happy with the farming practices of many of his neighbours; in his view, the bountiful orchards of the Okanagan hide many cancers caused by the over-use of chemical sprays.

Not all farmers who switch to organic farming are concerned about their health, but many of them make the change because they realise that the health of their soil is being damaged. Heavy doses of fertilizers and chemicals often reduce soil micro-organisms and earthworms which normally provide both organic nutrients and good soil aeration. No matter why farmers decide to farm organically, they all eventually discover that it just *costs* less to farm without chemicals. One farmer who found this out is Elmer Laird, who farms a section of land in Girvin, Saskatchewan, a small community midway between Regina and Saskatoon.

Laird grew up on a farm near Swift Current, southwest of Regina; he has been farming for 37 years. His wife, Gladys, also grew up on a farm. Like many older people, they can recall a time when farmers still used horses both for plowing and for transportation and when life on the farm was physically punishing. Laird used to work another three-quarter section, but he recently sold it to the provincial Land Bank because it was difficult to get help to work it.

Land prices have escalated; in 1960, Laird paid ten thousand dollars for one-half section of land—but an entire section of land here can now sell for as much as $400,000. Elmer Laird takes pride in his independent approach to farming and this is evident in his cheerful banter about the farm economy and the behaviour of most farmers. "There are two types of farmers," he says with relish. "Millionaires who own two sections of land and machinery—and the person who owns a million dollars' worth of land and owes one and a half million dollars on it."

Like all farmers, the Lairds have had their financial problems and it was an effort to save money that made them cut out chemicals fifteen years ago. Laird explains that in 1965, he attended an agricultural conference in Saskatoon where experts encouraged farmers to "grow all you can." Farmers followed these directions—and three years later, there was a glut of grain on the market and prices fell. Because he was feeling the financial pinch, Laird decided to cut out one major expense: chemical sprays. At that point, it didn't matter to him if he ended up with a poor crop; he already had all the grain he could pack into his bins. As it turned out, he didn't get the dramatic drop in yield that farmers usually expect when they go off chemicals. Now the Lairds grow wheat and rye with rotations of sweet clover to help add nitrogen to the soil.

The fact that it costs less to farm organically is crucial for younger farmers, who have high start-up costs for land and machinery. Also young farmers who are interested in conservation and soil improvement are often willing to start out with a lower class of farmland that they can build up over time. When Bart Hall-Beyer began farming in Quebec, he already had some rugged farm experience behind him; he had once taught farming at a residential school in the Yukon, and that job prepared him for the challenge of farming in the Eastern Townships. "I can afford the land here," he said. "If you are young and have little money, you are forced into marginal areas. If I hadn't farmed in the Yukon—forget it." Their debt load is moderate; his partner, Monique Scholtz, admitted that while she does not like being in debt, she is "not uncomfortable" with the $30,000 debt load carried by the business. Besides the mortgage, they have a three-year loan to pay for a truck, a loan to buy a few other pieces of farm equipment and some money they borrowed to buy a few heifers. They are on good terms with the bank; Bart points out that bankers respect well-organised farms. He explained that "if you tell them about your cash-flow problems ahead, if you show them you are on top of it and have done your homework," they will be more sympathetic if the farmer has trouble in meeting payments. Income on this farm comes from several sources because it is a mixed farm, raising livestock and self-sufficient in poultry. Although they have been short of cash, they were able to start raising hogs because they had helped an ill neighbour raise his pigs; in thanks they received several gilts—female pigs that have not been bred. The neighbour then "lent" them his boar and they soon had their first litter of piglets on the farm.

While their approach to farming may look piecemeal to some, both farmers know they could not afford to farm any other way. That kind of realism has kept them in business—in spite of the fact that their course instructors told them they would need to make a huge financial investment to farm commercially. "They used to tell us in ag school that you needed $200,000 to start in farming," Monique said, still astonished. "Some of us used to sit there and scratch our heads. That's a quarter of a million dollars!" While other students accepted high start-up costs as a fact of life, Monique didn't go along with it. "According to the *Wall Street Journal*," Bart said, "a beginning farmer in the United States now needs $800,000 capitalisation [to start up]!" That kind of assumption has gotten many farmers into serious financial trouble.

Other organic farmers who started out with little money and poor soil have similar stories to tell. Russel Pocock farms near Compton, off Highway 147, just south of Sherbrooke, Quebec. Ten years ago, he bought sixty acres of farmland which had not been worked for years. For the first five years, he did not raise crops on the land; he earned his living elsewhere while he worked at building up the quality of the soil through green manuring. It took time, but eventually, his small farm did well enough to receive both a grant and a low-interest government loan to help with renovations and farm equipment. The farm now makes money growing thirty vegetables and five acres of strawberries organically; they hire three to four people a year to help them. "That is my response to people who assume there is no money to be made in farming—especially in organic farming," says Pocock. "Down the road, there was a four-hundred acre potato farm that this guy got from his dad as a graduation gift. He laughed at me because of what I was doing. Now he's gone bankrupt. And we are surrounded by hog farms; they are desperate, having a hard time making ends meet."

Still, organic farmers have to look after their finances just as carefully as any other farmers. The attitude of bankers toward organically-run farms ranges from interest and curiosity to skepticism. One farmer, who told me his gross income was "well into five figures," said the bank had no problems with what he was doing. Some older organic farmers have already paid off their mortgages and do not want—or need—much assistance from the banks. Occasionally, bank managers are interested in lending money that the farmer has no interest in borrowing. Tony McQuail, for example, who takes out short-term loans to run his horse-powered farm is often offered more extensive credit that he neither wants nor needs for his low-cost operation.

Organic farmers get into financial trouble, too. Three years ago, Dave Reibling's organic farm and mill in Ontario was feeling the squeeze of the rising costs and a drop in sales. Reibling believes that had he been using chemicals, his farm would not have survived. "The bank manager told me, 'forget it,'" he said. " 'Start selling your assets because you won't be here a year from now.' " Reibling managed to pull through; he thinks his bank manager has now become "more tolerant" of the type of business he runs. "He has since told my accountant, 'I think they are going to make it; in a year, they'll be all right,'" Reibling added. His business is prospering, and his brand-name products are now available in many Ontario stores, but it was touch-and-go for a while.

Organic or chemical, all farmers have to deal with the problem of low income. "Michael Jackson can bring in two to three billion dollars for people who pay to sit in a seat from two to three hours," Dave Reibling remarked, "but a rise in the price of food makes people angry." He does not blame the urban consumer, though. "[The consumer] is our life-blood," he continued, "We're working hard to get them." But he is not surprised when shoppers get annoyed at farmers' demands. "The farmer is supplying such crap," he added with frustration: a consumer who has to buy stale, chemically-treated produce is not likely to sympathise with farmers who want higher prices.

Organic farmers have a better chance of getting a fair price for their products, because they do not usually deal with the giant corporate middlemen who normally get the largest share of the food profits. Organic farmers market their food individually or as part of a small group or co-op, and while this system has its limitations, it has allowed access to a specialty market which includes fine restaurants, health-food stores and local grocers. One grower remarked that her local grocer will pay premium prices for her vegetables because he sells them all and never takes a loss. It is also common for some smaller farms to do a custom business for rural neighbours and city people who place direct orders for eggs or livestock. Others make money selling at the farm gate. In British Columbia, organic food co-operatives buy from farmers who can also sell to markets in Washington state; the Canadian Organic Producers' Marketing Co-op in Saskatchewan is working to develop markets for their organically-grown grain. Similar farm co-ops operate in the Maritimes, and in Quebec's Eastern Townships, a small association of farmers sells to a US wholesaler who has a good market for lettuce and spinach which cannot be grown in the hot summer climate of the southern states. Not all organic produce ends up with an "organic" label in a specialty store. In Ontario, some growers end up selling their produce through the Ontario Food Terminal, the province's major food wholesaler for shops, supermarkets and restaurants—a bonus for the buyer who may randomly select produce grown without chemicals.[9]

If shoppers are willing to pay premium prices for organic products, there needs to be some reliable guarantee that crops or livestock are, in fact, raised without chemicals or feed additives. Over the past few years, a number of co-ops in Canada have tried to set such standards for their members with limited success. In Europe, a standardized certification system exists; it is the model for a system of standards for organic farmers which may soon be in place across North America. The International Federation of Organic Agriculture Movements (IFOAM) helped establish the certification procedure in Europe, where commercial organic farms have a greater degree of public acceptance. Recently, the Organic Foods Production Association of North America met in Toronto; fifty delegates representing organic farmers, processors, wholesalers and retailers agreed on the ground rules for a certification system that can be enforced by the regular inspection of organic farms.[10] Similar systems are already in place in the United States; Canadian farmers who sell organic food can become certified by an association set up by two of the larger wholesale groups.[11]

On the face of it, this is a promise of better things to come for the marketing of organic foods. Groups such as the US-based Progressive Agri-Systems attract many farmers with their expertise in organic production and marketing. Or is this only the new-age middleman, about to come between the farmer and a decent income? Organic farmers will have to learn to be skeptical of newcomers to the business who are looking for ways to earn money from organic food without actually producing it.

Organic farming may seem the sensible alternative for the farmer who wants to ease his debt load and save his soil, but many worry about a drop in yields. This is a real concern, especially since some crops suffer when the chemicals are withdrawn. In 1977, the Rodale Research Centre in Pennsylvania began a research study comparing crop yields on organic farms with those on conventional farms in their state. Farmers worked 320 acres of land near Kutztown, Pennsylvania, which had been treated with almost no synthetic fertilizers or pesticides since 1973. Throughout the study, researchers took soil samples and kept careful records of crop yields and the costs of running the farm. They grew alfalfa and red clover hays, corn, soybeans, and small grains, including barley, oats, rye and wheat over five growing seasons.[12] The completed study was then reviewed by five independent scientists at several US universities. It showed that crop yields at the test farm over the five-year period were the same or better than the country or state averages for those same crops. The average costs of production for growing those crops was ten percent below the cost of raising them on a conventional farm; in some cases, production costs were as much as thirty percent lower.[13] Martin Culik, an agronomist with the project, explains that the high yields were the result of an orderly system of crop rotation which returned nutrients to the soil and boosted fertility. Because of this, Culik is convinced that farmers do not have to settle for smaller crops when they make the transition to organic farming.[14]

In Canada, a recent survey of organic farmers showed that those who make the switch often start with smaller crops which increase in size over time as the nutrient balance in the soil is restored. Over half the farmers surveyed said that their crop yields dropped when they started farming organically. Many of them pointed to poor soil conditions and weeds as the problem; very few of them blamed the drop in yields on insects. The survey indicates that it takes about five years before crop yields return to their former levels.[15] Some of the farmers I visited know from experience that it is easier to start out in organic farming than to make the transition later. Louise and Jacques Charron own an organic farm and greenhouse complex in a secluded spot near St. Charles-sur-Richelieu, about an hour's drive east of Montreal. When they started farming eight years ago, they had no experience with greenhouse culture and they could not find anyone who could show them suitable organic techniques. They decided to start out raising their tomatoes and cucumbers with chemicals; they did this for four years before they decided to make a change. Three bad crop years followed. "We almost lost the farm," Louise told me. "But the chemicals had made the soil unbalanced and we decided that if we couldn't do it without chemicals, we'd sell the farm."

When the Charrons went to the bank to borrow money to replace a greenhouse roof that had caved in, they were refused a loan. "The bank manager told us, 'if you were chemical farmers, we'd give you the money, even if you had gone three years without a profit,'" she told me. The Charrons managed to borrow money from other sources; last year they had a good crop and earned back all their costs. "We did it the hard way," Louise admitted, "following chemicals with organic farming. The transition is very hard; it takes three to five years." It was made even more difficult because greenhouse crops are among the hardest to raise organically; the warm, humid environment inside a greenhouse is a good breeding ground for insect pests and fungi. The Charrons are now using a predatory wasp to keep down the insect population. But she advises greenhouse growers who want to stop using chemicals to do it gradually by changing over one greenhouse at a time.

Taking the transition in small steps also makes sense for fruit growers, who have come to rely heavily on a variety of chemical pesticides. Francine Lemay and Gaetan Choquette are directing this changeover slowly on their farm near Sherbrooke, Quebec. They own 196 acres of land which they have farmed for the past five years; both of them grew up on farms and are able to make a full-time living raising apples, raspberries and cereal grains. Like the Charrons, these farmers also wanted to start out growing fruit organically, but they had no information on how it was done. They began with chemicals, but three years ago, they started to discontinue the use of herbicides in their 2,000-tree apple orchard. Two years ago, they switched from insecticides to a type of flypaper which helps them catch and identify the predators in their orchard. Now they are gradually cutting back on the use of fungicides and other sprays. "We are supposed to use from eleven to fifteen different sprays on apples," Francine told me. "Now we are down to three." They do not spray their raspberries; in the summer, they run a pick-your-own operation where they tell customers which fruit are grown organically and which have been sprayed. Francine added that some of the fruit grown without sprays gets infested, but they don't lose money because they don't have to cover the expense of buying chemicals. In general, organic fruit growers find this to be the case.

If the experience of these farmers is any indication, it is hard to believe that many farmers would want to make the transition to organic farming when they get so little information. Most farmers learn about new developments in agriculture through the extension branch of their provincial agriculture ministry or through short courses sponsored by agricultural colleges. This information in turn comes from research conducted at federally-funded research stations. University agriculture departments also undertake research sponsored by both public and private funds. Farmers, like other professionals, try to keep themselves up to date, discussing new techniques with their ag rep before they try them out. If organic techniques were to be fully researched and promoted, there is no doubt that they would become more credible in the minds of many farmers.

We also need more research to determine how well Canadian climatic and soil conditions would support adequate food production using organic methods. A federally-funded research station for field studies of organic techniques would have a major impact. Universities with agricultural colleges could also do this research, but at a time when government funding is tight, perhaps farmers and other citizens should think of setting up a foundation to attract funds for research into alternative agriculture. Scientists and organic farmers might establish their own research station, similar to the Rodale Research Centre in the United States. When I visited Al Sheresky on his farm in Saskatchewan, I asked him if he thought his neighbours might adopt his style of farming if there were more research to prove how well it works. "This is what is needed," he said. "An experimental farm. Farmers listen if the university tells them that this type of farming works. Otherwise they won't try something new—unless it's tested first." In the meantime, Agriculture Canada is beginning to take notice of the good news that organic farmers do not go bankrupt[16]—a point which will also interest the taxpayer if the federal government were to fund research in alternative agriculture.

There's much to learn. A new organic farmer needs to know about weed and insect control, about the complex cycles of crop rotation which are required on a modern organic farm. Once he gets his farm under way, he needs to keep up to date. Some organic farmers are unhappy because their tax dollar is funding research into conventional agriculture, from which they get no benefit. Many told me that their local ag rep could not provide them with information on organic techniques and had little interest in non-chemical agriculture. This isn't always the case: the *agronom* in the Beauce region south of Quebec City is reported to have said that "my best producers are all organic producers."[16] Most ag reps try to help, but often they end up giving standardised guidelines on chemicals. "A lot of people spray out of fear," one farmer told me. "The Quebec government recommends [the herbicide] 2-4 D for berries, so guys just get their recipes and follow them. Farmers who will think independently of the *agronom* and who will blaze their own trail are a disappearing breed."[17]

The one notable exception to public indifference is the Quebec government sponsorship of the *Fermes Temoins*, selected organic farms which have been studied by researchers over a five-year period. The idea came from officials in the Quebec Ministry of Agriculture who responded to pressure from farmers for more research after the 1980 USDA report. One organic farm is being studied in each region of the province; the farmer keeps records for the study, including accounts, production methods and records of crop plantings and yields. In return, the ministry pays the farmer a small fee for his assistance. But farmers are dissatisfied with the programme: one man told me that his farm has been under observation for three years, but the ministry sends in different students each summer to work on the study. Usually, these employees have no background in organic farming. The problem is a lack of funding to manage the programme effectively; no one is employed full-time to oversee the entire study and analyse the data that the farmers are recording.[18]

No Canadian university has a research programme in organic agriculture. However, the agriculture school at McGill University has the most comprehensive resource centre on organic farming in the world. Ecological Agriculture Projects at MacDonald College is essentially a library housed in a space donated by the university. The centre was set up in 1974 by Dr. Stuart Hill, an entomologist and one of Canada's most prominent supporters of organic farming. It was established through a special grant made by a private foundation and it operates on other grants and private donations. This Canadian resource, little known to the general public, has a well-established reputation throughout the world. Government and university researchers from many countries make use of books, journals, videos and thousands of articles in EAP's collection dealing with organic farming, renewable energy, rural development and related topics. Staff members also give advice and prepare reports for government bodies and private organisations.

Research and resources are necessary, but it all comes back to the farmer. For years, I've heard farmers state over and over again that they simply cannot farm without pesticides. These are not people who deliberately try to damage the soil and create pollution. They reject a more sustainable method of agriculture because they have learned how to farm from bank managers, provincial agricultural specialists, chemical companies and farm machinery firms. Farmers are the targets of intensive advertising and they are just as susceptible to a good sales pitch as the rest of us. Farm magazines and newspapers are full of ads for state-of-the-art chemicals and machinery; local TV and radio stations run commercials for pesticides which the farmer can't miss. Some astute farmers recognise what is going on and they don't like it. Elmer Laird told me that he is concerned about advertising and how it affects the Saskatchewan farmer who is desperate to make money from his crop and who usually spends a lot of time alone with his worries. "You have to realise that the farmer on a tractor is isolated," he explained.

"He has the radio on in the cab and the commercial comes on, telling him to 'use Roundup and kill that weed!' And he looks down—and there's the weed. And he thinks 'get it!' But the ads don't tell him what that chemical does [to his health]."

Along with product advertising, many family farmers have been sold a set of ideas and values which have damaged the enterprise of farming in this country. This includes the belief that today's farmer can only survive if he treats the farm as a capital-intensive industry which consumes resources without replacing them. A more sustainable form of agriculture is bound to help the family farmer who stands a better chance of making a good living by cutting costs. It is even possible that the hardships farmers are facing now may accelerate the process of change to organic techniques. Ken McMullen, the President of Canadian Organic Growers, is convinced that "in twenty to fifty years, you will see [organic farming] on every farm in North America."[19] Whether or not this eventually occurs, a network of small-scale ecological farmers is now beginning to develop across Canada. Even if their numbers remain small, they are starting to create an alternate agricultural system which could have a considerable impact on food consumption. By increasing the demand for locally-grown food, organic farmers can help create regional markets. A demand for local products will help farmers develop distribution systems, allowing them to compete with imports. While proponents of large-scale agriculture argue that organic farming threatens the food supply, more lethal dangers to our food system may come from our growing dependency on imports to feed ourselves. Eventually, these options may include urban agriculture, which is already being practiced in certain areas of the country.

Many of Canada's organic farmers believe that the future will prove the value of their work. It is for this reason that they do not vociferously oppose the techniques of their farm neighbours. They speak about farming as a way of life, a business, a stewardship of resources, a skilled craft, a practical science and an art. They do not see it as an industry, but they do not spend time arguing with those who do. "We are not here to protest," said one organic grower recently. "We are here to set an example. We are the future."[20]

10
The City and the Media

However farmers may decide to help themselves, there remains justified suspicion that urban people are simply not interested in farmers. In the fall of 1982, the International Monetary Fund held a major gathering in Toronto; at the same time, an alliance of left-of-centre organisations opposed to the lending policies of that body held a counter-conference in the city. One of the participants, a well-known Canadian economist, addressed the subject of a new economic strategy for the province. At no point in this discussion was agriculture mentioned, in spite of the fact that it is the basis of a $5 billion industry in Ontario. Later, I spoke to the economist and I asked him where he saw agriculture fitting into the strategy he had outlined. He paused and looked thoroughly perplexed. "To tell you the truth, I really don't know," he said finally, with a trace of chagrin. He didn't try to invent a theory on the spot, and I respected his candor. Still, at this conference, farm troubles involving exploitation in the Third World were discussed in depth.

I have never met urban people who are openly hostile to farmers. But the gulf between them is broad and it deserves a much closer look than we usually give it. Rural communities were built around agriculture, which is not only our oldest collective activity, but also our most basic one. While farm techniques have altered dramatically over time, the farming cycle has never changed; farmers still plant in spring, harvest in fall and worry about the markets and the weather. The lives of urban people are not as deeply influenced by these cycles, and agriculture and its round of necessary chores often looks boring and unsophisticated to them. The family farm itself represents values which an urban person may respect but not understand. Cities have always been the homes of many people whose families left the country to make a better life for themselves; on the other hand, many farms represent those families which have chosen to stay together over generations in order to co-operate in a common enterprise. This may help explain why many farmers assume that we should appreciate what they have done for us; they see their stability as a social anchor which has a moral value the urban lifestyle cannot match. From this point of view, it is easy to see why the collapse of family farms feels so devastating to their owners; when the place disappears, gone with it is a family's sense of permanence and worth.

Closely allied with this is the farmer's real fear of negative stereotypes, since many feel that city people still regard them as hayseeds in coveralls who raise a few chickens and cows in the barnyard. Like racial minorities, farmers are justifiably sensitive to the way they are sometimes portrayed in the media. I have met many farmers who feel stigmatised by the image, often well-educated people who needed college training to help them get started with their highly-mechanised farms. There are positive stereotypes, too—and for a good reason. Many Canadians are themselves only a generation or two removed from the farm; for them, the country remains a symbol of renewal and peace, the sign that nature endures, however changeable their urban environment may be. The knowledge that farmers live as stewards of the land gives many people a sense of hope, and it is not a question of false nostalgia, as some farm leaders think. Last year, one of these leaders became annoyed by the portrayal of a clumsy old farmer in a TV cereal ad. The image was a cliché, but what this contemporary farmer had to offer in its place was no better. We were told that it would have been more accurate to show today's farmer dressed in a three-piece suit, riding in the cab of a state-of-the-art tractor. No one seemed to feel that the image of a noisy agrarian industrial park full of pin-striped suited farmers was not an especially comforting one.

The media has a major role to play in helping urban people understand farm issues. Very often, the problems farmers face make the most sense when we can see their connection with broad social problems—unemployment, inflation and urban sprawl, for example. Both urban people and farmers badly need this larger perspective on farm issues which well-researched media coverage can provide. Unfortunately, reporting on agriculture is usually restricted to bankruptcies, famines and dust storms on the one hand, and the more restricted "market news" in the rural press, on the other. Many local TV and radio stations cover farm news, but they narrowly address a rural audience. For years, CBC television has broadcast the *Country Canada* programme —a good documentary programme on farming which has been consigned to a Sunday afternoon slot. CBC Radio reports farm news every day on its noon-hour programmes; the *Radio Noon* show for which I worked in Toronto is part of this chain of regional "farm" broadcasts. Each of these pro-grammes has one or two agricultural commentators to cover farm news, with the exception of Newfoundland, where the noon show deals with fisheries instead. Similarly, the noon programme in Vancouver covers the range of resource indus-tries in British Columbia. What is common to all of these programmes is the broadcast of market prices for grain, livestock and other commodities, a feature which draws many rural listeners who might not otherwise tune in.

Ambivalence toward agriculture at the CBC began some time ago. Farm programming got started in the first place because of the pressure of farm lobby groups who rightly felt that farming had to be included if the network was to be a real mirror of the country. In the early days of farm broadcasting, radio was also the only means of providing isolated farm communities with essential information. This is the origin of the farm market reports—a feature which often exasperates producers because it is so difficult to keep urban listeners' attention while commentators read columns of numbers. That information is still vital for today's farmer, even though the widespread use of computers may one day make the markets redundant.

At the same time, farmers once were served by a very specific type of reporting, geared to everyday farm needs— the sort of information which is now dispensed by government extension offices. Because of this approach to the farm broadcasts, the CBC used to require that its farm commentators either have a farming background or an agricultural education. The programmes were friendly and informative, but steadfastly steered clear of the controversial issues. Implicit in all of this was a belief—apparently shared by both farm groups and the CBC—that agriculture was to be exempt from the standards of "mainstream" journalism.

Gradually, all of this changed; by the 1970s, young farm people who wanted careers in broadcasting often wanted to get away from farming altogether. And as Canada became more urbanised, the folksy style of farm broadcasting lost its appeal. The CBC realised that farm programmes would only keep their audiences if farm broadcasters were allowed to behave as journalists, rather than as chatty "over-the-back-fence" commentators. Initially, some farm organisations reacted to the switch, mistaking the change in style and emphasis for a lack of concern about agriculture. To deal with some of this negative feedback, the CBC made use of its Agriculture Advisory Committee;[1] this body is made up mostly of rural people who prepare reports evaluating farm programmes and including suggestions for changes.

While such committees can be useful, I had one early encounter with them which made me wonder if they were, in fact, a privileged pressure group within the system. I had been at *Radio Noon* only a few months when our unit was invited to lunch with this committee. Between mouthfuls, I was politely but insistently questioned about my qualifications for the job I held, since I had no farm background at all.

This was something new for me to contend with; up to that point, I thought that journalistic skills ought to be enough for a job as a journalist. I made it through that brief inter-rogation, and nothing more was ever said to me about it again. To the best of my knowledge, CBC no longer has any strict "farm background" requirements for farm commenta-tors. It is only fair to add that the initial reactions to "hard journalism" and non-farmers on the air disappeared, as farm groups learned that they could use on-air interviews to raise issues and reach the urban listener.

The future of the noon programmes looks uncertain. With budget cutbacks and a growing urban audience, much of the serious farm reporting has been replaced with more "upbeat" consumer stories. Whatever happens to the noon-time farm shows, there is little evidence that other CBC current affairs programmes have an ongoing interest in farm news stories. There are many areas in agriculture and agri-business which badly need to be investigated and exposed, and I have occasionally wondered if we are dealing with an unconscious but real urban prejudice against rural people when we define the majority of our news coverage as "urban" news. To my mind, this sort of ghettoizing is far more pervasive and disturbing than the corny TV ads that irritate farmers. I am aware that the same criticism can be made about news coverage of all people with rural lifestyles, including native people. But as far as farm broadcasting is concerned, those of us in the cities who want to meet the farmer half-way still have quite a distance to go.

We badly need a rural-urban dialogue, but most of us are not in the business of telling the farmer how to farm. However, there is an alternative and a meeting-ground, one which allows urban people a chance to show the farmer that they have a genuine interest in the value of his work. Whatever we may think of large-scale farming, we can learn from the farmer by becoming more socially responsible; rather than accepting the role of passive consumer, we can also, to a limited degree, become farmers ourselves.

A person who decides to provide some portion of his own food supply is also taking responsibility for a portion of

Canada's food self-reliance. Like the farmer who takes the initiative, the city person who grows food is reclaiming a sense of power—in this case, to exercise control over a food supply normally run by multinational corporations. Urban agriculture may involve nothing larger than a backyard garden; it can also mean the use of every available inch of yard-space for home food production—a fact of life in some ethnic neighbourhoods in Montreal, Toronto and Vancouver. In fact, the latter city now boasts an organisation set up to teach residents how to grow their own food: "City Farmer" was started by Mike Levenston, a man who got involved in urban farming while working on a federally-funded energy research project.

In an effort to find out how to reduce the energy used in food production, Levenston started to look at some of the small-scale alternatives. Vancouver had a head start in urban farming; he pointed out to me that he had once lived near the Chinese area of the city, where 90 percent of the people had traded lawns for vegetable gardens. Eventually, Mike Levenston and his research group pooled their own funds to start a small newspaper and a non-profit society, both called City Farmer. Gradually, local people got involved; the group made contact with members of Vancouver's city council, and they set up a public education programme with speakers who had experience with urban farming.

They now run short courses with talks given by agronomists who can advise city people on how to raise food. While they have never had any government funding, Levenston has had help and free publicity from the B.C. Ministry of Agriculture, which has provided several guest speakers. The group also runs a Demonstration Garden in Vancouver's West End, located behind the city's Energy Information Centre. Local people who want to get involved in the garden can learn how to grow crops, raise the food and take home their share of what they produce together. City Farmer is now planning for Vancouver's centennial in 1986—when they plan to set up demonstration gardens throughout the city, designed for special urban needs—including a rooftop garden and a garden for the handicapped.

Mike Levenston believes that urban farming could translate into big savings and good crops. He explains that a study by a city farm group in the US shows that a six hundred square foot plot of land (about twice as big as a good-sized backyard garden) can produce as much as 540 pounds of produce—depending, of course, on the length of the growing season. That is the equivalent of one pound of food per square foot of garden, or a total of $450 in savings on food bills (after the capital costs of setting up the garden have been paid). City Farmer would like to see Statistics Canada do a similar study on urban farming in Canada and how it might help city people financially during periods of inflation and high unemployment. Mike spoke enthusiastically about the idea of urban growers setting up an Office of Urban Agriculture in each of the country's five major cities, staffed by local people who know the region's soil and climate.

Since one-third of all Canadians live in just three cities, Levenston believes that community groups run by local residents could help many more people produce their own food. Vancouver is a city with high unemployment and a privately-run food bank; Mike Levenston believes that urban farming is a way to help hungry people meet at least some of their food needs. "I don't like to talk in terms of crisis," he explains, "but I guess we are preparing for a time when there *is* a crisis. We get eighteen years of education, but we learn nothing about food production—and this is the most important factor in our lives. Every school should have a garden. Urban agriculture has not yet taken off because we have always had lots of food and we've always been eating well. You only see urban farming coming in during an economic crisis, or with the Victory Gardens we had during the war."

Some people have criticised city farming by arguing that it could put rural farmers out of work. But Levenston doesn't see it that way. "We are working *for* farmers," he said emphatically. "When you learn what goes on behind the shelves in the store, then you take more of an interest in farmers. But as a rule, we are taught to be consumers only, and not producers."

Urban agriculture, like any other type of farming, has to start with good-quality soil. Vancouver is surrounded by prime farmland, but Levenston explained that Vancouver's soil quality is uneven because the earth layers got disturbed as areas were developed and building foundations dug. In these cases, topsoil can end up below the surface, while various subsoils get pushed toward the top. It is hard to know exactly what the city's soil profile is, but in Levenston's view, Vancouver's soil can be improved: "The compost you could create for your garden in this city is so amazing—why, we have wastes in this city from all over the world!" He continued, in a more serious vein, "We could be building the finest non-eroding farmland you've ever seen." However, livestock manure is often a big part of farm compost and most Canadian cities have outlawed raising small backyard animals. In Australia, cities allow livestock under certain regulations, and Levenston says Canadian cities would do well to study these rules more closely.

While the idea of urban agriculture may seem unlikely to many people, there is no reason why some of the waste space in urban areas could not be turned over to food production. In fact, this is already happening in some cities where land is rented out in garden allotments. Some of these gardens fill an important local need. In 1984, a group of people, mostly single mothers, planted a successful community garden in Toronto's Regent Park, an area with one of the highest concentrations of low-income people in Canada. The garden gave them plenty of food and a sense of pride in their ability to feed themselves and their families.[2] There is a growing number of hungry people in many of our larger cities; seventy-five cities now run food banks to assist them.[3] The larger problem of unemployment won't be solved by community food production. But for many people who are out of work, the ability to raise food together could offer them a sense of independence which the tight economy has taken away.

Urban agriculture may help city people; farmers may see them as unwelcome competition. It is hard to imagine that urban farming would ever put rural agriculture out of business. In fact, food production in the city plays an important part in educating the urban person to take a practical interest in agriculture. In talking to radio listeners, I gradually realized that those city people who take a serious interest in the survival of agriculture are also people who produce some of their own food. For them, it is a case of taking an interest in a political issue which feels as close to home as more "urban" concerns. By taking part in food production, they have made the farmers' concerns their own in a way they could not do as passive consumers.

The hands-on experience of urban farming could also be presented to young people as a part of a much-needed programme in agricultural education. Most provinces do not teach agriculture in the schools; one exception is Ontario, where farm groups have successfully persuaded the provincial government to include a unit on agriculture in the Grade 9 science curriculum. Some of the proposed course material I have seen looks quite informative and well thought-out. If you are old enough to remember studying agriculture in the public school system, you may find it hard to believe that many urban students have never seen a farm. The fact that they will now have this opportunity deserves praise, along with the Ontario people who lobbied for agriculture in the classroom. What disturbs me is the fact that nothing in this course material encourages students to become responsible adults who provide food for themselves. One brief on the subject comments that " 'Agriculture in the Classroom' does not mean vocational agriculture or teaching how to farm (others are taking care of that job.)[4]"

The "others" happen to be those professional institutions which train commercial farmers. The inference is that the rest of our young people are to be trained as good consumers, without any sense that can be active players in society who can take responsibility for part of their food supply. If this turns out to be the case, then the student who learns where food comes from will also learn the political lesson that he is meant to be a passive consumer, both of food and of information about food. In a similar vein, the same brief on the course emphasizes that no political point of view will be promoted in the classroom[5] — a statement which is naive and untrue. In the guidelines for the study of farming in Ontario's Middlesex County, one statement explains that "the concept of specialised farms should be stressed. Old MacDonald's farm lives, for the most part, mainly in the memory."[6] While no one wants to promote a primitive style of farming, it is unfortunate that these proposals do not mention the ecologically-sound idea of the mixed organic farm; they could also be included in student farm tours. The hidden agenda of agribusiness dominates this course proposal, which stresses "consumer awareness" of agriculture as an industry. Instead of educating young people this way, we can offer them the option of controlling one of the most important aspects of their daily lives. Whether or not they ever decide to grow food, kids can learn directly about the importance of agriculture by experiencing it, just as they learn about the importance of science by conducting experiments in the lab. In this way, they would also find out that food production is a social and political act as well as a personal one.

Farmers are right when they say that we take our abundant food supply for granted. We are a lucky country in that relatively few of us in Canada have ever known the meaning of hunger, and like it or not, the subject of food does not rouse the emotions that would move us to take political action. With the constant reminder of our North American food surpluses, there is little real reason to expect that we should. The image of abundance is as dominant in our culture as hunger is in parts of Africa; unless we have some other motivation for our concern about the farmer, we are not likely to take action until the cupboard is bare. Because of this, farmers have made a mistake by assuming that they have a ready-made political constituency just because everyone has to eat. Even a serious farm concern like low beef prices does not draw out attention; taken alone, it is too remote from most peoples' experience to matter to them.

Yet we are living through a period in history in which we are being forced to take a difficult look at some of our most basic assumptions about the value and uses of technology. Agriculture is a central part of a social dilemma which involves the future of our planet. As we become more aware of our environmental problems, it is hard to believe that we will be able to continue our costly system of agriculture indefinitely without ruining both our farm families and the soil they farm. We need to keep our farmers in business earning a fair living, and we need to do it in ways that will provide real long-term benefits—by developing sustainable methods of agriculture that will rebuild and conserve the soil for generations to come. Broad objectives such as these touch on all our lives; they will bring together farmers and city people more readily than any others. And these goals remind us that the regeneration of agriculture is not a private business concern; it is a social movement of great importance, one which lies at the heart of the broader movement for planetary survival. As such, it invites us to take part not just because we all eat, but because in some sense, we are all farmers who feel our responsibility for the care and protection of the earth.

Notes

Preface

[1] Interview with Mark Waldron, Director of Continuing Education, University of Guelph (CBC *Radio Noon*; Toronto: 8 February 1985).

[2] *Ibid.*

[3] J.D. McCuaig and E.W. Manning, *Agricultural Land-Use Change in Canada: Process and Consequences* (Ottawa: Lands Directorate, Environment Canada, 1982), p. 6.

[4] Hon. H.O. Sparrow, *Soil at Risk: Canada's Eroding Future.* A Report on Soil Conservation by the Standing Committee on Agriculture, Fisheries and Forestry to the Senate of Canada (Ottawa: 1984), p. 59.

[5] Dr. Edward W. Manning, "Farmland: The Myth of Plenty," *Bridges': Explorations in Science, Technology and Social Studies*, Vol. 1, No. 3, Feb. 1984, p. 10.

[6] *Ibid.*

[7] Eugene Ellmen, "Farm Bankruptcies," report for Canadian Press wire service (Toronto: 25 January 1985).

[8] Kevin Cox, "Bankruptcies Among Farmers at Fifty-Year High," *Globe and Mail*, 19 December 1984. Also, "Ontario Lost 154 Farmers," *Cobourg Star*, 31 January 1985.

[9] Kevin Cox, "Farm Bankruptcies Rise Highest Where Subsidies are Richest," *Globe and Mail*, 17 October 1984.

[10] Oliver Bertin, "Financial Ills Continue to Plague Agriculture," *Globe and Mail/Report on Business*, 14 September 1984.

[11] Kevin Cox, "Farm Bankruptcies . . . " *op. cit.*

[12] Letter from Mel Swart, Ontario NDP Agriculture Critic, "Squeeze on the Farmers Far Worse than Banks Say," *Toronto Star*, 6 Feb. 1984.

[13] Oliver Bertin, "Rising Costs and Falling Prices Extending Farm Income Slide," *Globe and Mail/Report on Business*, 25 January 1985.

[14] Dell O'Brian, Agricultural Advisory Council of Ontario in an interview on CBC *Radio Noon* (Toronto); 11 September 1984.

[15] McCuaig and Manning, *op cit.*, p. 4.

[16] Sparrow, *op cit.*, p. 4.

1. Ontario's Farm Crisis

1 The Hon. Dennis R. Timbrell, Ontario Minister of Agriculture and Food, "The Red Meat Plan," Toronto: 5 January 1984, p.6.
2 Oliver Bertin, "Ontario Ends Beef Agency Plan in Face of Cattlemen's Protests," *Globe and Mail/Report on Business*, 5 Feb. 1985.
3 Gord Wainman, "Church Group Supports Farm Marketing Boards," London, Ont.: *The London Free Press*, 29 June 1984, p. A6.
4 Lorne Slotnick, "Revenue Canada Tells Farmers When They're Not in Farming," *Globe and Mail*, 17 March 1984.

2. Wine and Milk

1 David Miller, "Ontario Wine Caught in a Squeeze," *Toronto Star*, 28 April 1985.
2 Tony Aspler, "Taste Test Shows Ontario Wines Can Hold Their Own," *Toronto Star*, 28 April 1985.
3 Miller, *op. cit.*
4 Nicholas Hunter, "Ontario Cautious on Wine Makers' Appeal to Lower Prices," *Globe and Mail*, 18 September 1984.
5 Miller, *op. cit.*
6 *Ibid.*
7 "Ottawa, Ontario to Buy, Store Grape Surplus," *Toronto Star*, 31 August 1984.
8 Miller, *op. cit.*
9 Gary L. Fairbairn, *Will The Bounty End? The Uncertain Future of Canada's Food Supply* (Saskatoon: Western Producer Prairie Books, 1984), pp. 78-9.
10 Brigid Pyke, "Marketing Boards: A Producer's View," *Kingston Whig-Standard Magazine*, 11 September 1982.
11 *Ibid.*
12 "Producer Milk Quotas," Ontario Milk Marketing Board Industrial Relations Division, Mississauga, Ont., 1984.
13 *Ibid.*
14 Lorne W.J. Hurd, "The Canadian System of Milk Marketing," An Address to the Michigan State University Milk Marketing Seminar, 28 July 1982, p. 12.
15 "Producer Milk Quotas," *op. cit.*
16 Hurd, *op. cit.*, pp. 18ff.
17 "Milk Pricing," Ontario Milk Marketing Board Industrial Relations Division, Mississauga, Ont., 1984.
18 Pyke, *op. cit.*
19 Hurd, *op. cit.*, p.2.
20 *Ibid.*, p. 29.

[21] "The Ontario Milk Marketing Board's Quota Exchange System," OMMB Information Brochure; Mississauga, Ontario: 1980.

[22] Pyke, *op. cit.*

[23] *Ibid.*

[24] Statistics drawn from "The Function of the Ontario Milk Marketing Board," OMMB Information Pamphlet, Mississauga, Ont.: March 1984 and Pyke, *op. cit.*

[25] Pyke, *op. cit.*

3. The Grain Belt

[1] "Drought on Southern Prairies Seen as Threat to Farm Survival," *Toronto Star*, 27 July 1984.

[2] John Miner, "Cruel Hand of Nature Hits Prairies Again," *Toronto Star*, 27 July 1985.

[3] "Prairie Farmers to Get Federal Aid," *Globe and Mail*, 8 Nov. 1984.

[4] Hon. H.O. Sparrow, *Soil at Risk: Canada's Eroding Future.* A Report on Soil Conservation by the Standing Committee on Agriculture, Fisheries and Forestry to the Senate of Canada. (Ottawa, 1984), pp. 46-7.

[5] *Ibid.*, pp. 45-6.

[6] "Saskatchewan Wheat Pool: A Co-operative," pamphlet prepared by the Communications Division of Saskatchewan Wheat Pool (Regina: 1983), pp. 11-12.

[7] John Spears, "Canada Target as US Wages War Over Wheat," *Toronto Star*, 10 March 1984.

[8] *Ibid.*

[9] Barry Wilson, *Beyond the Harvest: Canadian Grain at the Cross-Roads*, Saskatoon: Western Producer Prairie Books, 1981, pp. 171-3.

[10] *Ibid.*, p. 169.

[11] Interview with Wayne Easter; Saskatoon: 29 September 1984.

[12] "Surviving the Drought" (editorial) *Globe and Mail*, 3 Aug. 1984.

4. B.C. Fruit Growers

[1] Conversation with Ian Thompson, trade analyst for Agriculture Canada (12 June 1985). He explained that in this case, the US Commerce Department set an average "dumping margin" against the four B.C. co-ops named in the suit; the average duty was close to two and a half percent of the value of the berries when they are sold. But individual co-ops could, in fact, pay much less.

5. Bankers and the Farm Crisis

[1] Oliver Bertin, "More Help for Farmers as Loans Plunge," *Globe and Mail/Report on Business*, 31 December 1984.

[2] "Saskatchewan Bill to Stave Off Foreclosure of Farm Properties," *Globe and Mail*, 5 December 1984.

[3] Ronald Anderson, "Farmers are Experiencing Worst Time Since the '30's," *Globe and Mail/Report on Business*, 21 December 1984.

[4] *Ibid.*

[5] Farm Credit Corporation,*1984 Farm Survey* (Ottawa: 1984), pp. 8-9.

[6] Anderson, *op. cit.*

[7] "Economic Trends in Canadian Agriculture," Report by the Canadian Bankers' Association, Toronto: October 1984, p. 12.

[8] Oliver Bertin, "Farmers' Debt Load Up While Net Worth Drops," *Globe and Mail/Report on Business*, 13 September 1984.

[9] CBA Report, *op. cit.*, p. 12.

[10] Kevin Cox, "Bankers Review Sad State of Farming," *Globe and Mail*, 2 November 1984.

[11] CBC Radio News, 8am, 3 February 1985.

[12] Interview with tobacco farmer Hugh Zimmer, 13 August 1984.

[13] Letter from Mel Swart, Ontario NDP Agriculture Critic, "Squeeze on the Farmers Far Worse than Banks Say," *Toronto Star*, 6 February 1984.

[14] "Budget Gives Farmers Little of What Wanted," *Globe and Mail*, 24 May 1985.

[15] Cox, *op. cit.*

[16] Conversation with Daniel Lavoie, Farm Credit Corporation, Ottawa, 6 February 1985.

[17] "Farm Review Boards to Get Wider Mandate," *Globe and Mail/Report on Business*, 11 December 1984.

[18] John Spears, "Can We Afford to Let Farmers Go For Broke?", *Toronto Star/Business Today*, 3 November 1984.

[19] John Spears, "Study Shows Full-Time Farmers Getting By," *Toronto Star*, 20 October 1984.

[20] *Ibid.*

[21] *Ibid.*

[22] Oliver Bertin, "Rising Costs and Falling Prices Extending Farm Income Slide," *Globe and Mail/Report on Business*, 25 January 1985.

[23] Interview with Wayne Easter, President, National Farmers' Union in Saskatoon; 29 September 1984.

6. The World Market: Imports and Exports

1 Agriculture Canada, "Challenge for Growth: An Agri-Food Strategy for Canada," 9 July 1981.

2 *Ibid.*, pp. 4-24.

3 Edward Alden with Mauro Vescera, "Thorns of Plenty," *Harrowsmith* #58, Dec. 1984—Jan. 1985, pp. 38-40.

4 John Warnock, "Canadian Grain and the Industrial Food System," a paper prepared for the Conference of Learned Societies, University of Guelph, 10 June 1984, p. 21.

5 *Ibid.*, p. 10.

6 *Ibid.*, p. 10.

7 Dan Morgan, *Merchants of Grain* (New York: Penguin Books, 1980), pp. 43-4.

8 Don Paarlberg, "Food As A Foreign Policy Tool," paper presented at the Annual Meeting of the American Association for the Advancement of Science, Toronto; 6 January 1981.

9 James A. McHale, former Agriculture Secretary for Pennsylvania, in an address to the Christian Farmers Federation of Ontario, 3 April 1979.

10 Quoted in Morgan, *op. cit.*, p. 147.

11 Sociologist Harriet Friedmann, in J. Kates, "Uncle Sam Designs the Menu," *Globe and Mail*, 12 January 1984.

12 Warnock, *op. cit.*, pp. 9-15.

13 *Ibid.*, p. 12

14 Alden and Vescera, *op. cit.*, pp. 43-9.

15 Morgan, *op. cit.*, p. 192.

16 The National Report of the Peoples' Food Commission Hearings, *The Land of Milk and Money* (Toronto: Between The Lines Press, 1980), p. 41.

17 Alden and Vescera,*op. cit.*, p. 48.

18 Quoted in Alden and Vescera, *op. cit.*, p. 49.

19 *Ibid.*, p. 40.

20 Warnock, *op. cit.*, p. 23.

21 *Ibid.*

22 "Support for Farmers;" Statement of Policy of the Preservation of Agricultural Lands Society (PALS), St. Catharines, Ontario, p. 2.

23 *Ibid.*, p. 2.

24 *Ibid.*, p. 3.

25 Oliver Bertin, "Agriculture Harvests Crop of Raised Tensions," *Globe and Mail*, 13 Aug. 1984.

26 Oliver Bertin, "US Hog Tariff Seen Despite Past Failure to Benefit Producers," *Globe and Mail*, 10 June 1985.

27 Oliver Bertin, "Trading Subsidies Serve No One, Mayer Tells US Meat Exporters," *Globe and Mail*, 14 June 1985.

28 Oliver Bertin, "Farmers' Futures Placed in Doubt as US Raises Pork Import Tariffs," *Globe and Mail*, 12 June 1985.

29 Bertin, "US Hog Tariff . . . ", *op. cit.*

30 Bertin, "Trading Subsidies . . . ", *op. cit.*

31 *Ibid.*

32 Oliver Bertin, "Beef Import Quota Abandoned," *Globe and Mail*, 14 June 1985.

33 John Spears, "US Threatens to Cut Imports of Ontario Tobacco," *Toronto Star*, 11 September 1984, p. Cl.

34 *Ibid.*

35 Frances Phillips, "Imasco Keeps Up Drive to Change Product Mix," *Financial Post*, 5 May 1984.

36 John Spears, "Tobacco Growers Seek Marketing Agency," *Toronto Star*, 29 December 1984.

37 *Ibid.*

38 "Tobacco Industry Seeks Break in Taxes," *London Free Press*, 6 April 1984.

39 Gord Wainman, "Tobacco Heyday Feared Thing of the Past," *London Free Press*, 6 April 1984.

40 Interview with Hugh Zimmer on CBC *Radio Noon*, Toronto; broadcast 23 April 1984.

41 Robin Harvey, "Tobacco Tax Called Blood Money," *Toronto Star*, 13 April 1985.

42 Ronald Labonte, "Folly to Aid Tobacco Farming," *Globe and Mail*, 18 April 1985.

43 Chris Thomas, "Tobacco Growers Seek Alternate Crops," *The Simcoe Reformer*, 4 May 1984.

44 Zimmer interview, *Ibid.*

45 John Spears, "US Threatens . . . ," *op. cit.*

46 _____, "Tobacco Growers . . . ," *op. cit.*

47 The recent offer of the R.J. Reynolds Company to purchase Nabisco Brands is a good example. Reynolds, a diversified company best known for cigarette production, is clearly setting its sights elsewhere in order to increase its profits.

48 CBC *Radio Noon* report; Toronto, 16 April 1985.

49 "Ontario Companies Aid Tobacco Farmers," *Globe and Mail*; 30 October 1984.

50 Harvey, *op. cit.*

51 Labonte, *op. cit.*

7. Corporate Agribusiness and the Cheap Food Policy

[1] Two thoroughly documented papers contain substantial research on this subject. See John Warnock, "Canadian Grain and the Industrial Food System," a paper prepared for the Conference of Learned Societies, University of Guelph, June 1984, and Brewster Kneen, "From Agriculture to Agri-Food," a paper delivered at the Conference on Science, Technology and the Maritime Small Farm at St. Mary's University, Nova Scotia, March 1983.

[2] S.M. Lipset, *Agrarian Socialism* (Berkeley: University of California Press, 1971), pp. 84-6.

[3] "In the First Place, Should You Speculate?," (Chicago; Conti-Commodity Services, Inc., 1980) pp. 13-14.

[4] Wheat producers in Canada avoid this situation, unless they sell feed wheat; it is illegal to speculate in wheat for human consumption, which is sold to the Wheat Board.

[5] "Understanding the Commodity Futures Markets," (New York: Commodity Research Publications Co., 1975), pp. 19-21.

[6] *Ibid* ., p. 22.

[7] Dan Morgan, *Merchants of Grain* (New York: Penguin Books, 1980), pp. 276-80.

[8] *Ibid.*, pp. 280 ff.

[9] "The Commodity Futures Link in the International Food Chain, Who Needs it and Why Most of Us Don't," (Toronto: GATT-Fly, 1977) p. 21.

[10] Morgan, *op. cit.* pp. 280-81.

[11] "The Commodity Futures Link . . . ," *op. cit.*, p. 24.

[12] "Potatoes: Canada's Troubled Staple Food," (Toronto: GATT-Fly, 1982); pp. 2, 6.

[13] Dean Walker, "McCain Foods: Branching Out on a Spud-Spangled Strategy," *Executive* Magazine, Dec. 1983 reprint.

[14] *Ibid.*

[15] *Ibid.*

[16] "A Regional Overview of Land Use Policy as of March 1984," included in *For Land's Sake*, a study kit prepared by the United Church Standing Committee on Agriculture and Food Resources. (Toronto: Canec Publishing, 1984).

[17] Conversation with Wayne Buffet, a New Brunswick Agriculture Ministry official involved in negotiations for the national potato agency (8 July 1985).

[18] Conversation with Joe Rideout, General Manager, New Brunswick Federation of Agriculture, 8 July 1985.

[19] Wayne Buffet, *op. cit.*

[20] Conversation with Mr. B.A. Fredstrom, Public Relations Director, McCain Foods Ltd., Florenceville, New Brunswick, 8 July, 1985.

[21] "Potatoes: Canada's Troubled Staple Food," *op. cit.*, p. 4.

[22] "A Regional Overview . . . ", *op. cit.*

[23] A policy which was explained to me by Eric Hammill, Secretary-Manager of the P.E.I. Federation of Agriculture, 8 July 1985.

[24] Conversation with Mr. Jack Desroches, Public Relations Director for Cavendish Farms, 8 July 1985.

[25] Mr. Hammill, *op. cit*.

[26] Mr. Desroches, *op. cit.*

[27] Mr. Hammill, *op. cit.*

[28] *Ibid.*

[29] Mr. Desroches, *op. cit.*

[30] These percentages are derived from census data:
Statistics Canada, *1981 Census: Agriculture/Canada*, Cat. #96-901, Table 34, "Farm Data Classified by Type of Organisation".
_____, *1971 Census: Agriculture/Canada.* Cat. #96-701, Table 31,"Type of Organisation for Census Farms, by Province".

[31] *Ibid.*

[32] Percentages derived from census data.

[33] " . . . And Then There Were None;" A report on family farming in Ontario by the NDP Agricultural Task Force, March 1984, p. 10.

[34] Edward Alden with Mauro Vescera, "Thorns of Plenty," *Harrowsmith* #58, Dec. 1984—Jan. 1985, p. 50.

[35] The National Report of the Peoples' Food Commission Hearings *The Land of Milk and Money* (Toronto: Between the Lines Press, 1980,) p. 50.

[36] NDP Task Force, *op. cit.*, p. 11.

[37] Garry Hewston and Daniel Pearen, "Canadian Food Retailers," *Farm Market Commentary* (Ottawa: Agriculture Canada, v. 4, #1, March, 1982), pp. 22-27.

[38] Derived from statistics quoted, *Ibid.*

[39] *Ibid.*

[40] Pamela Cooper, "Foreign Ownership in the Canadian Food and Beverage Processing Industries," *Farm Market Commentary*, (Ottawa: Agriculture Canada, v. 3, #1, March, 1981), pp. 10-15.

[41] Hewston and Pearen, *op. cit.*

[42] *Ibid.*

[43] Lawson A.W. Hunter, "Buying Groups," *Farm Market Commentary*, (Ottawa: Agriculture Canada, v. 5, #4, December 1983), pp. 15-18.

[44] *Ibid.* p. 15.

[45] Peoples' Food Commission, *op. cit.*, p. 43.

[46] Agriculture Canada, "Challenge for Growth: An Agri-Food Strategy for Canada," 9 July 1981.

⁴⁷ Kneen, *op. cit.*, pp. 10-11.
⁴⁸ *Ibid.*, p. 11.
⁴⁹ *Ibid.*, p. 7.
⁵⁰ Elbert van Donkersgoed, "The Future of Family Farming in Ontario," notes for a speech to the Niagara South Pork Producers' Association, 15 Feb. 1985., p. 7.
⁵¹ Quoted in *The Ram's Horn*, farm newsletter published by Brewster and Cathleen Kneen, Scotsburn, N.S. (Aug., 1984).

8. Networks and Co-ops

¹ The following information about the CFA was given to me by David Kirk, the organisation's Executive Secretary (24 June 1985).
² Interview with Wayne Easter, President of the National Farmers' Union (Saskatoon, 29 Sept. 1984).
³ "Farm Policy for the '80s: 1984 Policy Statement of the National Farmers' Union" (Regina, 1983), pp. 26-30.
⁴ Comment by Harry Pelissero, President of the Ontario Federation of Agriculture, quoted by CBC reporter Tom Egan on *Radio Noon* (Toronto: 10 July 1985).
⁵ M. Zafiriou, "The Impact of Labour Cost Increases on Food Price Inflation, 1970 to 1982," *Farm Market Commentary*, (Ottawa: Agriculture Canada, v. 6, #3), Sept. 1984, pp. 35-44.
⁶ Allen Wilford, *Farm Gate Defense* (Toronto: NC Press Ltd., 1984), p. 205.
⁷ Interview with Wayne Easter in Saskatoon, Sask., 29 Sept. 1984.
⁸ "Doesn't Anyone Care About Plight of Farmers?", Letter of Bob Cote to the *Toronto Star*, 15 December 1984.
⁹ NPI Policy Statement in *The Ram's Horn* (Scotsburn, Nova Scotia, January 1985), p. 3.
¹⁰ Conversation with Brewster Kneen, 24 June 1985.
¹¹ Conversation with Glenis Joyce, 25 June 1985.
¹² Interview with Brewster Kneen, Oct. 1984.
¹³ Northumberlamb information statement, February 1984.

9. Organic Farming: A Way Out

¹ Conversation with Tomas Nimmo, marketing manager for Oak Manor Milling, Tavistock, Ontario (13 August 1984).
² Le Mouvement Pour L'Agriculture Biologique (MAB) is also the name of Quebec's largest organic farming group.
³ Jerry V. Mannering, "What is Organic?" Crop and Soil Notes, *Indiana Prairie Farmer*, Summer, 1983.

4 Judy Stamp, "The New Agriculture," Toronto, *Probe Post*, June 1983, p. 15.

5 Jennifer Bennet, *The Northern Gardener*, Camden East: Camden House Publishing, Ltd., 1982, pp. 37-9.

6 A common complaint of many organic farmers who try to work land which has been treated with this chemical. Also, see Lill Ellison, "Sustainable Agriculture," Ecology Action Centre, University of Halifax, pp. 3ff.

7 *Report and Recommendations on Organic Farming*, prepared by the United States Department of Agriculture Study Team on Organic Farming, Washington D.C.; July 1980, p.6.

8 Kevin Cox, "Safety of Chemicals Queried Ten Years After Bogus Tests," *Globe and Mail*, 30 June 1983.

9 Interview with Ken McMullen at the Federal Hearings of the Consultative Committee on Industrial Bio-Test Pesticides, Toronto; March 1982.

10 David Cohlmeyer, "Organic Foods Industry Works on Certification," *Globe and Mail*, 27 February 1985.

11 Interview with farmer Russel Pocock, November, 1984.

12 M.N. Culik, J.C. McAllister, M.C. Palada and S.L. Rieger, *The Kutztown Farm Report: A Study of a Low-Input,Crop/Livestock Farm*, Regenerative Agriculture Library Technical Bulletin, Rodale Research Center, Kutztown, Penna., 1983, pp. 1-3.

13 *Ibid.*, p. 56.

14 Interview with Martin Culik at the Annual Conference of Canadian Organic Growers, Peterborough, Ontario, 23 March 1985.

15 Dee Kramer, "Problems Facing Canadian Farmers Using Organic Agricultural Methods," a paper presented by Canadian Organic Growers to the Pesticides Project of Friends of the Earth. Toronto: April, 1984, p. 39.

16 The president and two members of Canadian Organic Growers have recently presented a 170-page report called "From Frontier to Mainstream: Sustainable Agriculture in Canada" to the Strategic Planning Division of Agriculture Canada. The study was requested as a background paper documenting the growth of interest in organic farming techniques.

17 Interview with Russel Pocock, *op. cit.*

18 *Ibid.*

19 Comments made to the Canadian Organic Growers Annual Meeting, Toronto; November 1984.

20 Remarks made by McMullen at Canadian Organic Growers Annual Meeting, Toronto, Nov. 1984.

10. The City and the Media

1 This was not a move to single out farm broadcasting for public criticism; the CBC has similar committees to provide advice on science and religious programming.

2 Commentary by June Callwood, *Globe and Mail*, 12 October 1984.

3 Robert Sheppard, "Food Banks Called Sign Social Services Failing," *Globe and Mail*, 2 May 1985.

4 "Agriculture in the Classroom: Legacy of the Past; Challenge of the Future," researched and prepared by the Wellington (Ont.) Federation of Agriculture, Education and Public Relations Committee, 1984.

5 Especially since the provincial Ministry of Agriculture is listed as having co-operated with this brief. The point of view is implicit; issues such as land use and global food demand are suggested as topics of discussion, while structural problems in the economy that hurt farmers are ignored.

6 "Agriculture in the Classroom . . . ," *op. cit*, Appendix B2.

Index